NORFOLK FOOD HEROES

INSPIRATIONAL FOOD PRODUCERS & FAVOURITE RECIPES

STEPHEN BROWNING
& DANIEL TINK

HALSGROVE

First published in Great Britain in 2011

Copyright © Images 2011 Daniel Tink
Copyright © Text 2011 Stephen Browning

British Library Cataloguing-in-Publication Data
A CIP record for this title is available from the British Library

ISBN 978 0 85704 115 9

HALSGROVE
Halsgrove House,
Ryelands Business Park,
Bagley Road, Wellington, Somerset TA21 9PZ
Tel: 01823 653777   Fax: 01823 216796
email: sales@halsgrove.com

Part of the Halsgrove group of companies
Information on all Halsgrove titles is available at: www.halsgrove.com

Printed in Italy by Grafiche Flaminia

CONTENTS

DEDICATION

Daniel would like to dedicate this book to his fiancée, Ali, a wonderful cook.
Stephen would like to dedicate this book to his sister, Juliet.

THE AUTHORS OF THIS BOOK WOULD LIKE TO THANK THE FOLLOWING

Jane and Lesley-Anne Cargill of Foxley Wood Aberdeen Angus Farm; Shawn Grey and Paul Daniels, Cromer fishermen; Mike Thurlow of Orchid Apiaries; Peter and Jenny Burgess of Kitchen Gardens; Steve Childerhouse of Great Grove Turkeys; Liz Joint of Ebenezer Cottage; Rona and Philip Norton of Norton's Farm Shop; Grimsby, Sally and Rob of Pye Bakers; Sam and Bertie Steggles of Fielding Cottage; Glen Weston of Cley Smokehouse; The Forum Norwich. Finally, thanks to Simon Butler of Halsgrove for all your help and advice.

INTRODUCTION

A CELEBRATION OF THE WONDERS OF FINE NORFOLK FOOD

IF YOU ASK SOMEONE to name some famous Norfolk foods, they would probably not have any difficulty in coming up with sugarbeet, maybe, or turkeys, mustard or chocolate. If that someone was keen on history they may say 'Cromer crabs, Yarmouth bloaters and Caister dumplings'. This is all true, and yet there is so much more to the story, too.

Similarly, the area is blessed with some nationally famous names – Delia Smith, Galton Blackiston or Bob Flowerdew, for example. So, also have our festivals, events and markets – from the Whitebait Festival on the North Norfolk Coast in the last century to the present Cittaslow movement in Aylsham and the 'battle of the bangers' in Norwich each September – attracted the attention of foodies worldwide. And yet…

This book was inspired in no small part by a wander around the Bidwell/EDP Norfolk Food Festival. Here we saw the best organic veggies, ducks eggs, pork pies, Aberdeen Angus beefsteaks, artisan breads and cakes, fruits, juices, jams, pickles, butter, cheeses, milks, poultry, honey, lamb and pork, crabs, lobsters and vegetarian wonders.

It is fair to say that Norfolk is undergoing a transformation in its image to the extent that 'food tourism' is now a major player in the local economy. We had the idea of a visit to some of the best of our present generation of food specialists. We wanted to know: how were these fine foods made ready for market? Why, given the almost 24/7 nature of the task in some cases, did people do it? What made a farmer a farmer? What was the human story behind it all? There surely must be some magic behind the lifestyle? What is it?

Armed with a camera and notebook, we set out in a little silver car, oftentimes on foot across very long tracks and fields, to discover some of the answers. We have been to many

Vibrant locally-grown peppers.

parts of the county, fallen over in the mud, been rained upon heavily, had our trousers set upon by cows as big as buses, tasted the greatest mince pies in the world, discovered that kale does indeed get stressed, been pecked by screeching turkeys and much more besides.

It has been absolutely fantastic and everyone has made us very welcome. Thank you to all our 'Heroes' who invited us into their homes, farms and kitchens. We hope the joy of our odyssey (for such it seems, as we usually had no idea what we would find) comes across in these pages. And, along the way, some of our questions have been answered. Not all, but that is what you might expect as there is an alchemy, a wonderful unexplained something, in the best food, as in our marvellous 'Norfolk Food Heroes' themselves.

Stephen and Daniel
Norwich 2011

Opposite: A perfect quiche tartlet will have pastry that is fresh, crisp, slightly golden, and neither too sweet nor sour. It can be filled with virtually any prime Norfolk produce you desire.

MINCE
& STEWING STK
2 pks
:80 £6.00

FINE NORFOLK BEEF

JANE CARGILL IS A VERY busy lady. Daniel and I have come to talk to her and her daughter, Lesley-Anne, in her large farmhouse kitchen in Foxley Wood, and have just managed to catch her after another Farmers' Market. 'I do about 14 a month,' says Jane, settling us down with mugs of steaming tea. 'This last one was one of five in a row.' And the farm? Who looks after that when she is away? 'Well, there's me and my partner, Terry, and Lesley-Anne – Oh, and we employ someone to help with the cattle and other farm work.' The farm seems huge and it is difficult to believe that one smallish family can accomplish so much.

We have just come back from a tour of the magnificent Aberdeen Angus cows and bulls and it is these we have come principally to talk about. Daniel has taken some good pics –

Opposite: Jane Cargill and her daughter, Lesley-Anne, set out their stall selling prime Aberdeen Angus beef in the Forum, Norwich.

Prime Aberdeen Angus cattle at Foxley Wood Farm.

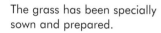

The grass has been specially sown and prepared.

the day is bright blue, the grass a luscious green and the cattle very friendly, especially one small calf who attempts to lick the camera to bits, apart perhaps from one magnificent beast which thinks Daniel's jeans taste delicious.

'So where does your family come from originally, Jane?'

'Scotland, Steve. My Father's family came down between the wars in the Depression, when lots of Norfolk land was being sold off cheaply. We had other land but came here in 2000 and have been building up the farm ever since. It was purely an arable farm – traditionally, Norfolk has been the bread basket of the country. Then, after two years, we made the decision to buy some cattle.'

'That must have been a momentous change. But how did you actually go about doing that?'

' You lookin' at me...?'

'Mmm... that sure tasted good!'

Jane smiles broadly at the memory. 'I will never forget how three of us from around here went to Salisbury where there was a herd of prime Aberdeen Angus cattle for sale, including cows in calf. We each bought some and drove them back in a huge two-storey cattle float arriving here at 1.30 in the morning. We turned them out into a field for the night and went to bed.'

'And the present herd – do they all originate from this first 'batch'?'

'Absolutely. From twelve new arrivals, ten calves were 'girls' and two 'boys', which was ideal. We did once think of having another bull but a friend of ours who was more experienced than us at the time in raising Aberdeen Angus cattle came to see us. He had a look at our two bulls and advised us that, as they were fine stock, to use them and not to possibly risk importing disease into the herd with a new arrival. So the herd is a 'closed' one.'

And what is the most popular cut? 'No doubt, at all – steaks. I get calls direct from restaurants for prime steak. I can sell steak blindfolded,' laughs Jane. 'On the whole, people don't want so much of the braising cuts which is a great shame: these cuts are a third the price of the steaks and make fantastic dishes.'

I think that most people have had experience of buying the cheaper cuts from their local supermarket and finding them almost inedible. I certainly have. I wonder if it is the cuts or the cooking? 'Well, both, possibly. It is incredibly important that the beef is hung for at least three weeks – four or five is even better. Natural enzymes in the muscle cells gradually soften the cell walls allowing them to relax and tenderize. Funnily enough, the meat will appear dryer to the touch but, when cooked, will be much juicier. A lot of customers are also very pleasantly surprised to find that our well-hung beef takes less time to cook than is the case where it has been under-hung. So you get your money back by buying the best. Norfolk folk are canny on the whole – they know you get what you pay for!'

And the cooking? How is that best done?

'Well, let me give you an exclusive recipe for the braising steak.' Jane goes over to the kitchen sideboard and rummages about in one of the drawers, emerging with some well-used pieces of paper. 'There is a recipe on here somewhere, if I can interpret all the squiggles and blobs and things!'

We broadly try the recipe as follows:

FOXLEY WOOD PEDIGREE ABERDEEN ANGUS CASSEROLE

'Tell you what, I won't give quantities as it can be done in thirty different ways and one of the beauties is that you can use whatever ingredients you like, from your garden or your favourite vegetables, maybe, in whatever quantities you please.'

Take the meat, cube it and dust with seasoned flour. Brown in a hot pan. Put into a casserole dish. Then take onions, carrots, turnips, whatever you fancy, and cook lightly for a few minutes in the pan. Put into the casserole dish. Then add some stock and herbs – whatever you like really – perhaps also add a tin of tomatoes. If you have a slow cooker you can cook it all day: if not, heat at about 180 degrees for 3 or 4 hours.

Lesley-Anne with one of her charges.

Co-author, Stephen, gets
to know the herd…

Maybe serve with jacket potatoes, or chips; maybe a fresh salad and chunky Norfolk bread.

The beauty of it is that it tastes wonderful and, if you have friends over, the host/hostess will not be hot and bothered!'

'And how do you look after the cattle? What skills are needed to keep them healthy?'

'Well, obviously you need to keep an eye on them and investigate any abnormal behaviour. Feed them a proper diet with adequate minerals and keep them clean. If they get a cut in their hoofs, for instance, and then the mud gets in, they can get an infected foot. Then we would have to give them give them antibiotics, but this is a rare occurrence I am glad to say.'

'What do they eat?'

'In the summer they are grazing. The grass is special. You remarked, Steve, on how green and rich it is: well, we planted all of that specially. In the winter, the cattle come in and their diet is grass silage and barley straw. Growing animals get an additional protein top-up. What's silage? We have a few fields where we plant a variety of grasses and lots of clover. We use the minimum of fertilizer and absolutely no chemicals. The clover helps create nitrogen which builds fertility in the soil. This grass is cut and stored for winter feed. At this time of year (Autumn) we introduce them to their winter diet, as you saw just now in the fields. There are extra rations for the young ones in the calf creeps during the summer.'

'Calf creeps?'

Jane's steak and kidney pie.

'Yes, specially constructed containers which are small so that only the calves can get access. Then we take them inside and the calves are weaned away from their mothers. Oh, the noise for about three days! Both mothers and offspring set up a perpetual racket of moos! Then all calms down.'

I have always been fascinated by animal 'language' – I had a much loved dog once and I swear he used to talk to me in various subtle ways, some of which I maintain I understood. I cannot resist asking Jane if the various types of 'moos' can be interpreted. 'Certainly, yes, some can', she replies, laughing. 'The moos when calves and mothers are separated are unlike anything else. Then there is another 'distress moo'. Again, a mother calling a recalcitrant calf who has wandered too far away is slightly different.'

'And the moos we heard today, when the cattle were happily grazing away. Can those be interpreted?'

Jane looks at me with slight forbearance. 'No, they are just moos.'

'Townies like us', chips in Daniel, 'sometimes wonder about the folklore of farming. Here we are, a long way from the road or any other buildings – in a lovely farmhouse kitchen, surrounded by outbuildings, chickens, cattle, fruit trees and acres of green, green grass: we could be in Tolkien's Middle Earth. Well, me and Steve did wonder about some folklore…'

'What', she says. 'are we talking about?'

'I did read,' I reply, 'that the countryside has special rituals and cures. For instance, in medieval times it was thought that if a child had whooping cough, he must go into a field where calves have been born and kneel down and eat three daisies making sure only his mouth touched the flowers. On the second day he would eat four daisies, and on the third, five. Then he would be cured. Or if a newly born baby had colic, then the baby must be taken into a field of cows and passed three times under the belly of a pregnant cow…'

'There is some truth in the saying that a cow will lie down when bad weather is approaching,' continues Jane. 'That is probably because they want a dry spot to lie down in when it rains. The rest… well I have an open mind…'

One of the nicest things we have seen in our visit is the affection between cattle and humans. Lesley-Ann, Jane's daughter, who will one day take over the farm, has a particular

Opposite: Succulent silverside from Foxley Wood Aberdeen Angus herd, cooked by Jane.

Foxley Wood Farmhouse.

favourite. When we enter the main field there is one calf who comes over to her for a nudge. Lesley-Ann throws her arms around his neck. It makes a lovely picture.

'This calf was sad and sorry when it was born. It was rejected by its mother,' Lesley-Anne continues. 'It was born three days before Christmas. It would have died but that we looked after it – almost like a human baby. One of us would have to lift it up. We had a chair and one of us would sit on the chair and feed it milk. It was about two and a half foot tall. It is a healthy, beautiful cow now. She produces great milk and wonderful calves.'

Jane looks down. There is something else to this story, isn't there?

'She rejects her own calves. She produces superb calves but when they are born she doesn't care for them at all. If one tries to suckle her, she will kick.'

What happens? 'She is such a wonderful cow', says Jane, 'that she will stand us coming in and milking her – with her calf, no halter at all – and we take the milk in bottles and feed it to her offspring. Then, her calf will wander around the various aunties and one will take her on.'

Cows are introduced to the bull at about two years old. They produce offspring about nine months later. 'And how long do you keep them for?' I ask Jane. 'About fourteen years. Some people keep them to produce calves at eighteen. We don't do that.'

'How do you know when they have had enough?'

'They will tell you. Maybe they will get arthritis, or they will get biffed by a younger animal. Then they may just lie down and give up. Vets will tell you that they just collapse and refuse to get up again.'

Daniel and I drive off slowly in the enveloping dark. There is a farmhouse over there somewhere and cows, clover and cattle doing whatever they do.

Back to the city – pubs and things.

CRAB POTS, LOBSTERS AND LIFEBOATS

IT IS POSSIBLE THAT, in 1901, Arthur Conan Doyle, unable to sleep well due to enteric fever, was pacing around his room in the Hotel de Paris at 4.00 in the morning and glanced out of his window toward the cold and beautiful sea. He was possibly thinking of the legend of the Black Shuck, told to him by some locals over his brandy the previous evening. Maybe, or maybe not, he then had the 'eureka!' moment, and decided to transport the legendary hound to Dartmoor. At all events, it was just a year later that possibly the most famous of all the Sherlock Holmes stories, 'The Hound of the Baskervilles' , was published. It was an immediate sensation all around the world and Cromer is where it was born.

Early light

There is something in the air at Cromer, maybe literally, that inspires, especially at 4.15 in the morning. We have come to watch the fishermen go out in the half light under a glowering sky. In particular, we have come to meet up with Shawn Grey and Paul Daniels. The boats will probably go out about three miles today and be gone for four hours or so. The sea is choppy and there is a blustery south-west wind, but nothing really to prevent the tractors successfully manoeuvring the boats into the water.

Shawn and Paul are part of the inshore fishing fleet which numbers about 14, not that they are all going out right now: just a couple at this minute – 4.26am. Daniel and I watch as the little crab boat recedes choppily from view into the vast Norfolk sea, until it is lost altogether from sight.

The Seasons

It is crab season now, being September. Some fishermen work all through the year nowadays, but most serious fishing starts in March. There are two types of pots used – the traditional pot from eons ago and the newer 'parlour' pots, so-named because a crab is enticed in and then falls into a separate parlour from which there is no escape. If you leave the traditional pots too long on the bottom of the ocean, the crabs will eventually work out

It is four in the morning. Paul, in the boat, and Shawn, on the tractor, get ready to launch under an angry-looking sky.

how to escape. Each fisherman has his own preference. As regards timing, the traditional saying is that crabbing goes on until Wimbledon tennis starts. Then lobsters replace the crabs for about six weeks and, thereafter, back to crabs again. The lobster price fluctuates wildly – at Christmas when there aren't many about, they can fetch £28 a kilo but during Wimbledon, when everyone is catching them the cost to the shopper plummets to £3–£4 a kilo. Canadian lobsters hit the cheaper supermarkets about then, too, at very low prices.

A walk and breakfast

About eight am, they are back. The catch has been good – lobsters and the famous Cromer crabs. There is a fair amount to be done, measuring, packing and getting the catch to

All has gone well. Shawn and Paul return with their catch after four hours at sea.

Shawn.

The catch must be transported as quickly as possible to waiting customers.

customers as quickly as possible. Eventually, Shawn suggests we go for a walk along the seafront to a café for breakfast. It gives us a chance to ask him about his life as a fisherman.

Shawn first went to sea when he was seven. He remembers the occasion very well. 'My Mum and step-Dad had a fisherman's cottage at the top of the gangway in Cromer. I can remember my step-Dad telling me to hurry up 'cause I couldn't find a sock! "Come on," he said, "get ready, get ready!" Funny how you remember things like that. It was dark when we went out . Drifted with herring nets, off Cromer. That was it, I was hooked! Once I'd tasted the sea at the age of seven, I never had any doubt what I would do in life.'

Do they still catch herrings? 'Not off Cromer. It was the big thing in those days. Today the modern cook doesn't have so much time for them, which is a shame. Funnily enough, I saw a stallholder selling some today – they came from Caister. But, no, it ain't a commercial thing really anymore. Fishing today is a dying trade. Years and years ago, you'd get father-to-son, father-to-son for years and years and years. But no, today, the young people don't seem to want to do it. Why? They want an easy pound.'

'It's hard work – it really is. Physically demanding, at times mentally demanding – you don't get no second chances. No disrespect, Daniel, but if I took you out now, you'd probably be ill. There are even days when I get sea sick – and I started when I was seven and will be 39 next birthday. I had a step-brother, John, and he would come sometimes and he was fine. But I was always sick – sick as a dog. But when it was really rough, it was always me what got took - not John.' Shawn laughs. 'You are going to ask me "Why?" aren't you? Well, I guess my step-Dad could see that it was always going to be *me* that would become a fisherman. How did he tell? No idea! But he was right, wasn't he? And it paid off, 'cause although we have a period between October and March when we don't fish, I have never been out of work.'

I wonder what the fishermen do in the off season. 'Well, you gotta make enough money in the season to tide you over when there's no fishing. In the old days there were lots of jobs you could get on the farms – like sprout picking. Now, times have changed – EU etc. We have to compete now with workers from all over. I have a family; four children with my wife and a step-daughter, she's 21, and a grandson, so quite a big family. I got bills to pay like everyone else and it's getting harder, but… there we are.'

In the off-season, too, there is a great deal to be done – nets, pots, boats, tractors (to get the boats out) and fishing gear all have to be maintained. 'If you put in the work in the off-season', says Shawn, 'come the spring, you will reap the rewards. If you do not do it, you'll pay for it, won't you?'

A mysterious something, and a close fraternity

It's evidently a hard life, so what is it that makes Shawn go back to the sea? 'It hooks you, it really does. Magic – yeh! And it's a way of life. I work with people, but not *for* them. I am my own boss. And fishing families all know each other; the fishing fraternity is quite close. It's surprising how interlinked the fishing families are. You've got the Gaffs – he's been going for 40 years plus – then you got the Davies family, then the Jonases and the Byewaters from Runton. Then you got the Daniels, who you already know – Paul is Charles Daniel's son, and you got a picture of him with a crab, yeh? They are all inter-related somewhere along the line! To be a real Cromer fisherman you have to come from a true fishing family.'

Daniel and I have previously paid a visit to Shawn's home and have met his wife, Emma, so I just have to ask him: 'And is your other half from a fishing family?'

The only way to get married...

'No, she isn't, but she is from a Norfolk farming family. We went out together at school. Then we drifted apart for a while but got back together Been together coming up to 14 years now.' A huge grin. 'Our marriage was a bit unique. She is the only bride to be took to Cromer Church in the inshore lifeboat! '

We both grin widely at the image. 'How did you manage that, then?'

'Well, I was lifeboat crew at the time. Yeah, I spent nine years on the crew. So we asked if it was all right for her to come to the church in a lifeboat! So there she was, the boat on a trailer, her in it and ribbons and so on, full crewed, slowly coming up the road to the church. It won't ever be repeated as they didn't want everyone to ask for the same thing. But, yeah, our wedding ceremony was unique! April 13th it was.'

Daniel asks *the* pertinent question: 'And does she ever worry about you? Going out to sea?'

'All the time. All the time. We are at the mercy of the wind and the tides.'

Cromer crabs and lobsters

'I know you said the herring industry is not really going anymore,' I say, 'but how about crabs and lobsters. Are they plentiful, still?'

The lobster catch must be inspected and measured.

'Not as much as they used to be, Steve. Fishing methods have become better. We catch more in a trip than maybe a hundred years ago. And the cost of things keeps going up. Bait, pots, fuel – it's all got much more, but the price of, say, a crab, has not. There used to be a saying that the price of a crab should be the same as a pint of beer. And what is that now? £3? Well, you won't get a prime Cromer crab for that these days. And you won't sell many live crabs anymore. If you present a live crab to the modern cook they will probably scream and run for cover as it scurries over the floor in their kitchen. No, it has to be prepared, put in a bag and offered with a plastic spoon. This all adds to the costs.'

'And what do you use for bait?'

'We use leftovers of cod, plaice and other fish, but the main thing is what we call 'horse mackerel', which is like mackerel but with more bones. Crabs like a pure food, but lobsters, well, the smellier the better. I have heard that lobsters are partial to aniseed, even firelighters! – strong smell of paraffin, you see – but if you have one of those on a romantic

Traditionally, the prime time to catch
Cromer lobster is during the six weeks
following the start of Wimbledon.
It is cheap then, but prices will
increase seven-fold towards
Christmas when they are not so
plentiful.

Paul holds a prime specimen
of the famous Cromer crab.

evening you might light your fire in a different way than you could imagine! I wouldn't recommend it!'

And the thousand pound question. 'Is the Cromer crab better than other crabs?'

'Of course, it is.'

A slight pause. Sheepishly, 'Why?'

'Why? – 'cause of the ground it has been feeding off. The texture is better, the flavour is better, the colour is better, the nutritional things are better. You go to a market today and, yes, you will see much bigger imported crabs and people will buy them. They look such good value for money. But that is wrong – you will get much more prime meat off the smaller Cromer crab.'

When Shawn was at school he used to take sandwiches and have lunch with his mates. They would ask each other what they had in their lunchbox. One would say 'jam', another 'luncheon meat', another 'cheese', but Shawn would say 'lobster.' He got them so often he would often swap one of his sandwiches for a jam one. 'They thought it was Christmas!'

Funny things
'Have there been funny things that happen on the boats?'

'Funny things, Daniel? Sure have been. Best laugh I probably ever had was a bit on the rude side, but here goes. One time I was out with Billy, off Overstrand it was. I was bending down in the boat measuring the crabs when Billy got a call. "Oh, no, Jim has broken down". Now, it's not that we don't want to help each other, but, honestly, when you've got your catch, all you want to do is get home and have your breakfast. Well, we went to him. There was three on the boat – Jim, Paul and Rusty. Rusty was being sick over the side, Jim was trying to stop laughing and Paul was standing there stark naked apart from his Bamskin – a sort of plastic apron – and his hat. Steering the boat with hardly a stitch on.

I said, 'Jim, Jim, what on earth has been going on?'

'Well, Shawn, we were not far out when Paul said he needed the toilet.'

'Need to go, need to go!'

You can't,' I said, 'just have to hold on.'

'Don't think I can.'

Shawn is having difficulty telling us this as he can't stop chuckling. He comes to the high point of the tale.

All of a sudden, with a look of horror, Paul says, *'Jim, it's too late!'*

'What do you mean?'

'Well, I strained when I picked this pot out the water and... I done it... I done it...'

'The only thing for Paul to do was to strip down to his string vest and he used that to clean himself up. So here he was standing in just his Bamskin and hat. He wasn't a young chap, neither, with his silver hair and white whiskers. He looked really funny. The worse thing of all was that the tale, of course, got round all the fishermen and Paul got a couple of incontinence pads sent him and one morning his tractor got wrapped in toilet paper.'

A catch of Cromer crabs.

'Another time, we were out in a crab boat and my mate always had wine gums with him. One time – blustery it was – he reached into his pocket for the last one and, all of a sudden, a blast of wind blew the empty wrapper over the side. Now, wine gums are sticky, aren't they? And we could see the wrapper with a £10 note stuck to it – 'cos Billy always kept his money in this pocket as well. Just before hitting the waves, the £10 note got separated and – Steve, Daniel – blow me down, a seagull swooped and flew off with it in his beak. Didn't bother with the wine gum wrapper! Billy was having none of it – we must have chased that seagull for 15 or 20 minutes. Never got the £10 back!'

More serious things

All the while we are talking, tales swing back from crab and lobster boats to lifeboats. Seems natural, somehow, although Shawn makes light of his life-saving excursions. There have been some sad times, inevitably, but, as with fishing, being part of the lifeboat fraternity is also in the blood. Earlier, Shawn told us about going out to sea and getting smitten when he was seven years old. Something similar happened with lifeboats.

'I can't remember how old, I was. Quite young. The slipway was being repaired and we had to take delivery of a Mercury Class boat for a while – you can launch them off the

A perfect example of the finest crab in the kingdom: the Cromer crab cannot be beaten for colour, texture and taste.

beach, see. We had to go and pick it up. So there we were, off the Monks at Happisburgh, bringing the boat back to Cromer. Now the Monks can be terrible – if the seabed is rough, the waves will be the same.'

Shawn remembers they had the Divisional Inspector on board, and things got so bad, they lost the railings and their aerials. 'Better go back. Go back. Can't get to Cromer in this,' said the Inspector.

Now the skipper, David, a legend now, had a big beam on his face – he liked a challenge. 'Can't do that. Can't.'

'Why not?'

'Not enough fuel. We have just enough to get into Cromer. He then shouted to me, 'Shawn, come up here behind me, grab hold tightly and *don't move*. OK?'

Shawn did as he was told and David set a direct course for Cromer beach. It was so rough that the church spire rose and fell from view. 'But, you know – Daniel, Steve – we got back and I never even got my jacket wet. David later told me it was the roughest sea he had ever seen.' A slight pause. 'It was an honour, a real honour.'

IS THERE STILL HONEY FOR TEA?

'I FEEL LIKE AN ASTRONAUT', Daniel says as he dons his white protection suit and makes exaggerated Neil-Armstrong-type giant steps over the lawn towards the bee hives with his camera.

'That's fine,' laughs Mike Thurlow in whose garden we are. 'If there's one thing bees don't like, it is sudden movement!' Mike gently takes the top off a hive all the while gently smoking the bees, an age-old practice that does no harm but calms them down. He lifts a tray vertically into the open to reveal an amazing amount of frenetic activity. 'These are Buckfast Bees, originally bred from the Abbey in Devon, renowned for their gentle temperament,' he explains.

We have come to Orchid Apiaries, run by Mike, and located in Surlingham, Norfolk. In addition to his hives in the garden, he has thirty apiaries scattered throughout Norfolk. A garden gate leads directly into the village churchyard with the striking octagonal church tower just a few yards further on.

'Look, you can see the queen,' Daniel, 'the one with the striking green markings.' I keep my distance in my role as official camera case carrier – I can see a few bees resting on Daniel's white suit. 'When I was younger I got stung by a bee,' I try to explain, 'and my hand came up like a football.'

'That would have probably been a Bumble Bee and not a honey bee,' says Mike. 'I am amazed that people get them mixed up.' Discretion being the better part of valour, however, I stay where I am.

Mike has had a very interesting life. He spent seven years in Africa and Botswana working as an engineer for De Beers. His love of bees, though, started at school where the boys were allowed to study and tend the hives. 'Not that we were ever allowed to process the

Mike working in his laboratory.

The white flakes are beeswax: the nasty little orange creatures are dead Varroa mites (adult size: 1-1.8mm long and 1.5-2mm wide).

honey, though.' He laughs. 'Just imagine what a messy thing we boys would have made of that!' His teacher, Mr Pavey, used to do all the bottling in the holidays and the pupils were allowed to buy a jar or two when the school term started again.

'So when you returned to bee-keeping, you did it for love?' I ask.

'That's right,' he replies. 'There's no such thing as a financially wealthy bee-keeper – not in England at least, but more than once at city markets I've been told "you have the best job in the world".'

Prior to becoming a full-time bee farmer, he spent a season as a bee inspector for the government. 'Some good experience but not for me though – too much time spent filling in forms...'

So, how much honey does he produce in a year? 'Maybe, in a good year, about ten tons. You have to be fit 'cos you have to carry that at least three times before it sees a jar. We have not had a good honey crop since 2006: the past four years have been poor.'

'I feel like an astronaut!'
Daniel in his protection
suit just prior to the bee
photo shoot.

Mike in front of one of the hives.

There are many different types of product – willow, ivy, heather, starflower, lime, to name a few. 'People are completely different in their tastes. In London I might sell dozens of jars of ivy honey at a trade fair. In Norfolk, I might not sell any. Ivy is quite strong.' Any general trends, though? 'Yes – over the last decade, folk have become much more discerning in eating generally and speciality honey with distinctive tastes have become much more popular. In London, I sell mostly strong-flavoured honeys, but in Norfolk people are conditioned to bland-tasting honey from the yellow fields of oil seed rape.'

I remember, when I was a nipper, loving 'crunchy' honey: marvellous on toast. Mike smiles. 'Most honey will granulate sooner or later, but some folk will actually throw it away thinking it has gone off. To keep it runny for a long time to suit the supermarkets it has to be strained very finely, usually at a temperature which destroys some of the honey's beneficial properties.'

Daniel is being very intrepid and taking pic after pic a few inches from the hive. Eventually, he is satisfied and we retreat indoors where Mike makes us tea, into which we spoon some willow honey – crunchy, naturally. I ask Mike about the honey-making year.

'I have to work with the weather and the bees and be ready to move quickly. I keep some bees permanently in Norfolk, but around early April I will get a standby call from Kent pear-orchard farmers (the flowering period is only 2-3 weeks). As the first blossoms open, I will move up to 150 hives, first to pollinate the pears and then the apples. In August we will take hives to the North Yorkshire Moors for heather honey unless the weather forecast is poor. Kings Forest in Suffolk can also be good for heather honey if the weather has been kind – about once every four years. Then it's back to Brecklands for ivy honey – we may get two tons in a good year.'

'I was telling a friend of mine from the Westcountry about our visit today,' I say to Mike, 'and he told me the following tale about when he was a young man. He was helping a beekeeper transport some bees – they used an old horse-box – for pollination. Well, all went well and they loaded the hives back on to the horsebox for the trip back. Apparently, the 'trick' was to do this in the early morning when the bees were a bit sleepy. Alas! About halfway home they had a puncture. During the fixing of the tyre, the bees woke up and were not at all happy! They got out through the nooks and crannies of the horsebox. All the way home – very, very slowly – the bees formed an angry swarm above the vehicles as they followed their hives. It must have been quite a sight and a bit frightening.'

Opposite: What frenetic activity!
A section of one of the hives.

'That sounds a bit hairy,' says Mike. 'Glad to say, that has never happened to me: we always close our hive entrances when travelling any distance!'

In winter the bees must be looked after with great care. They don't sleep but are in a comatose state, congregating in a large cluster, the inside temperature of which is about 30 degrees centigrade. 'They are hardy,' Mike says, 'and can exist in temperatures of up to minus 40 centigrade, provided they are dry and have enough food. If the weather is mild enough some may venture out to collect water.' But what, I enquire, do they eat? 'The best winter food is pure liquid carbohydrate: some honeys make poor winter stores. They don't need protein in winter. I use a special enzyme-inverted syrup which is placed in a feeder bucket on the top of the hive in Autumn – up to 30 pounds is needed for a large hive and the bees will transfer this to their combs.'

And the queen? 'She lays a few eggs in the winter, but not many. She will be looked after ready to be busy in the spring.'

And how, I wonder, are new colonies started. Is it something just left to nature, or does the beekeeper lend a hand? Mike explains: 'New queens are raised by what we call 'grafting'. This involves transferring larvae when they are a few hours old to queen cells where the worker bees feed them with royal jelly. These cells are placed in small hives to start new colonies. The young queen will leave the hive to mate with drones on the wing and a new colony will be established. Queen or worker, it's all down to how long the larvae are fed royal jelly – just a little bit of natures 'magic'.'

I am aware that many people consider that the health benefits of honey are very significant. 'This is an area that needs more public awareness and research,' says Mike. 'Dark honeys have more antioxidants than light. Some folk swear by the therapeutic qualities of honey for hay fever. I even know of one chap, now regularly playing cricket and in his seventies, who firmly believes that honey has controlled his stomach cancer, but, no, I have an open mind. One has to be very careful about making claims regarding the health benefits of honey.'

Daniel asks Mike if he has a special recipe he would like to share? 'Hmm…,' Mike says. 'I could give you a new honey but my bees need a year's notice for that! Tell you what, I have a nice recipe for honey cake. Try this.

Opposite: The queen can be clearly seen here as she is bigger than the other bees and has been marked with green paint to aid identification.

SURLINGHAM HONEY AND LEMON CAKE

Ingredients:
8oz plain flour
2 level teaspoons baking powder
6 oz butter
6 oz brown sugar
2 tablespoons Wherryman's honey
Finely grated peel and juice of one lemon
3 eggs

Method:
Preheat oven to 175C. Line a 7-inch round cake tin with greaseproof paper.

Warm the butter and sugar in a small saucepan.

Meanwhile whisk the three eggs and sift flour and baking powder.

Once butter and sugar are melted add the honey and lemon peel.

Pour this into a mixing bowl and mix in the eggs. Add the flour and beat briskly.

Finally mix in the lemon juice.

Transfer to the tin and bake in the centre of the oven for an hour or until well risen and golden, or until a cocktail stick etc. into the centre comes out clean.

Leave in the tin for 10 minutes before turning out on to a wire cake rack.

Carefully peel off paper.

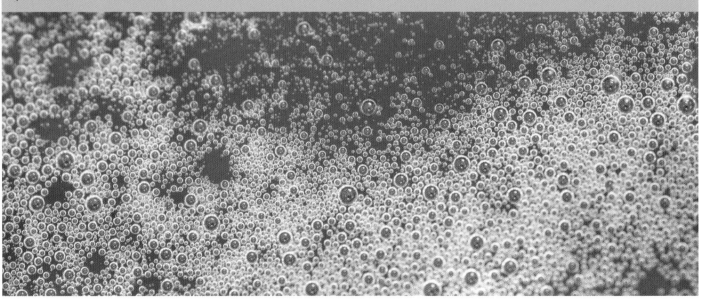

Mike also is pleased that some of the country's top restaurants use his honey for ice cream and puddings, wafer-thin slices of comb on top – delicious!

I am only too aware that the bee population is declining. It is often in the press. 'Varroa mites are one of the leading culprits,' Mike informs us. 'Come on, I will show you some.'

We cross the garden. The day has turned into a typical, soft, wet and very green Norfolk afternoon. The bees think better of getting out and are all in their hives. 'This is my workshop – and laboratory.'

Mike takes out a tray from a defunct hive. Spread across it are what seem to be tiny granules in various shades of brown and some white flecks. 'Look closely,' he instructs. 'The white flecks are wax but the nasty little orangey-brown creatures with their legs in the air are dead mites. They got into the honey bee population in Asia about 50 years ago – the native bees, *Ceranae,* are able to deal with the mites having thousands of years of practice. Honey bees, with our help, are slowly achieving some tolerance. In simplistic terms, the mites feed on the bees' blood and eventually the colony dies out.' Is there anywhere that the mites don't exist, I wonder? 'Yes, in Australia, but then they have very strict quarantine laws there.' And what is to be done? 'A lot more research is required!' Mike is understandably passionate about this. 'Our political masters may have their hearts in the right place, but the money is just not there! We need much more research from experienced entomologists.'

Mike also shows us, under a microscope, what different pollens look like. 'We can identify the floral source of any honey via the pollen grains trapped in the honey. You would be surprised at where some of the 'local' honey comes from.'

'And what, Mike, are the main types of honey you produce?'

'Got your notebook? Well, here we go – these are my main types:'

• Norfolk Blossom Honey. Each year this can be different depending on the weather and flowers around the apiary, but can include nectars from willow, fruit trees, dandelion, rape seed, sycamore and, in summer, bean, blackberry, lime, sweet chestnut and marshland flowers, as well, of course, as garden flowers where an apiary is located within flying distance of urban houses.

Opposite: I didn't realise that there were this many bubbles in honey! A close-up of a jar.

41

Mike 'smokes' the bees to make them calmer as we approach for pictures

• Ivy Honey. This is the last honey of the year, gathered in September and October. It has a strong aroma and granulates quickly.

• Cranwich Heath Honey. The bees at Cranwich pollinate many species of flower growing locally including wild raspberries which give this honey a fine flavour. It is slow to granulate.

• Beckhithe Honey. From the fringes of the Halvergate marshes, this spring honey is mainly from willow and blackthorn.

• Heather Honey. From the Brecks and also from the North Yorkshire Moors, this is jelly like, with a very intense flavour and needs a special process to extract it from the combs.

• Breckland Honey. An Autumn honey, this is dark with a strong aromatic taste.

• The Wherryman's Honey. The Wherryman's Way has recently received a big boost from Steve Silk's marvellous book for Halsgrove detailing walks along the River Yare. We were encouraged to provide this honey with its own identity. It is full of flavour, deriving from marsh flowers such as willow herb, figwort, purple loosestrife and balsam.

Unfinished business – Buckfast bees hard at work

• Starflower Honey. Borage, grown commercially, needs honey bees for pollination to obtain a good crop of seed, and this can be crushed to produce a very valuable oil. The honey, when pure, is pale (water white) in colour, with a sweet and delicate flavour.

It has been a wonderful day. We have one more treat in store. Mike produces an array of different honeys (some only produced once in every ten years) and some sampling spoons. Daniel and I try them all. Researching a book like this may be terrible work, but someone's got to do it! 'Favourites?' asks a grinning Mike?

'Willow, definitely,' I say.

'Nonsense,' replies Daniel. 'Heather honey – now that is *some* taste!'

THE RAF, VEGETABLES AND CYCLING UP HILLS

DOWN A WINDING COUNTRY lane, some six miles from Norwich, the Church of St Mary lets the visitor know that they have entered the tiny hamlet of Sisland, population 44. The church is a very unusual whitewashed building with a thatched roof, apparently built in 1761 on the site of the former church which was destroyed by lightning right in the middle of a summer Sunday service. It must have seemed like divine retribution in that highly superstitious age, which may account for the great haste with which the church seems to have been rebuilt using such extant bits and pieces of wall as were not too terribly charred. Inside it is beautifully cared for and is very important, being the only communal space in the hamlet.

Peter Burgess lives directly across the road where he grows 65 different types of organic vegetables, and some fruit, for distribution to customers through his Organic Box Scheme. Peter comes out to meet Daniel and I as we walk up to his front door. He is smiling broadly and looks very fit, which is hardly surprising as he explains when we go inside for a welcome cup of tea on a coldish, lowering Norfolk late morning.

'There's just me and my Mum, Jenny. We grow, harvest and deliver about 100 boxes a week,' he laughs. Jenny, a distinguished gardener of Alpine plants in her own right, puts the kettle on.

'You must need lots of holidays?' I suggest.

'No, no holidays', says Peter. 'We work 364 days a year.'

'What, only 364! That's a bit lazy, isn't it?'

'Well, Christmas Day, I try to take a few hours off, but even then I have to go out around the fields and check everything is all right. But you have to *care* for these crops. There is

Peter's Mum, Jenny, with some of her Alpine collection: she is an acknowledged national expert in the field.

Opposite: Peter and Jenny amongst some colourful squashes.

45

COURGETTE, CARROT & ORANGE CAKE

The following delicious recipe, using Peter's produce, has been created for us by Gemma Parker of www.humblecake.co.uk

Ingredients:
175ml/6floz sunflower oil
175g/6oz soft brown sugar or light muscovado sugar
3 eggs
75g/2½oz courgette, grated
75g/2½oz carrot, grated
110g/4oz sultanas
Zest of 1 orange, grated (save the juice for later)
175g/6oz self-raising flour, sifted
2 teaspoons mixed spice
1 teaspoon bicarbonate of soda

For the drizzle:
Juice of 1 orange
30g/1oz caster sugar

Method:
Preheat the oven to 180°c/gas mark 4

Grease a 2lb loaf tin and line the base with greaseproof paper

In a large bowl beat the oil, sugar and eggs together for 30 seconds

Stir in the courgette, carrot, sultanas and orange zest

Mix in the flour, spice and bicarbonate of soda

Pour the mixture into the tin and bake for 55-65 mins until when a skewer is inserted in the middle it comes out clean (i.e. with no wet cake mixture).

To make the drizzle; in a small saucepan, gently heat the orange juice and sugar until the sugar dissolves. Prick the cake all over with a skewer or fork and pour the drizzle over. Leave to cool

always something to be done, even after dark. In the summer I am up at five and work until 10 o'clock in the evening.'

'And how do you feel about it all?' asks Daniel. 'Do you ever get fed up?'

A huge grin spreads across Peter's face. 'Absolutely never. I am a very lucky man. Truly blessed. I'll show you around in a minute and you will see why.'

Peter probably inherited his love of the soil from Jenny. It is forty years since Jenny was driving up the lane on a Good Friday and saw the house for sale. 'I was looking for something I could do with children.' she explains. Peter was born in this house a few years later and went to school in Loddon. Jenny went to horticultural college and then worked for Daniels – now Notcutts – where she was in charge of Alpine and herbaceous plants amongst others. 'I also had a cousin who was a botanist, and the enthusiasm came from

Kales. The dark red one in the centre is 'Redbor'. On the left is 'Cavolo Nero'.

him really.' Peter's sister lives next door, not that she shares the passion. A loud chuckle – 'No, not at all. 'My sis works for the UEA. You won't see a fork or spade in *her* hand!'

Jenny continues: 'It has to be said, as well, that Peter was not always so keen as a boy, because every holiday we would go somewhere to inspect Alpines. But it was our life; we became a visitors' centre for them. Sometimes, we would be having Sunday lunch and a coach would arrive – we got used to seeing strange people wandering about the garden.'

'And now?'

'Now, although I still have many plants, I have really retired from the Alpine business. I help Peter – collector, packer, delivery driver and consultant!'

Peter breaks in, laughing: 'Yeah, she is invaluable if I have a problem. We can discuss it before deciding I am right all along…'

Peter at work in his fields.

Jenny produces a beautiful book, published a few years ago in which a chapter on the Alpine collection bears testimony to her expertise.

'Nothing was really planned – it just sort of morphed,' Peter explains. 'Morphing' is something that comes up a lot in the next few hours, as one thing seemed to just lead to another. 'I took over the vegetables when my Grandad died and, at first, it was a decorative thing really…'

'People would come to look at the Alpines', says Jenny, 'and see the vegetables and think "Hmmm, that's interesting…"'

This led to growing fine vegetables for family and friends, and then to the local WI. It was luckily at this time that Farmers' Markets became a big thing. 'It was fantastic,' Peter remembers. 'At our first market we were sold out within an hour. We had no sales plan or anything. It just grew and grew.'

And the Box Scheme? 'Yeah, well, we started with about ten customers who we got through the Farmers' Markets and now we've got a few more.' So what exactly is the scheme? 'Basically, it is a relationship between ourselves and the customer – you can't always get that in the bigger schemes. Each week we deliver a minimum of eight varieties of vegetables and a little fruit. It is picked in the morning and delivered in the afternoon.' And do the customers all get the same things? 'No, no… we get to know what they like or don't like and we substitute say, potatoes for pak choi, or whatever. It is all about getting the customer back in touch with the seasons and they can ask us questions like what does and does not go into it. A typical box would contain potatoes and carrots, a couple of different types of greens and some salad – this week it's rocket – and then maybe two more roots on top of that, maybe a swede and a parsnip, or onions.'

One of the best things about the scheme is that customers often become firm friends. Peter and Jenny get invited to weddings, christenings and all sorts of family celebrations. Three of the 'original 10' still receive a weekly box and many more have been around for years.

Tea over, we venture outside. We pass a number of greenhouses. One has Alpine plants, another fresh young salad seedlings and a third a pretty spectacular array of different squashes: a blue one called 'blue ballet'; a light yellow spaghetti variety; the buff-coloured butternut squash; a beautiful little green-striped type called 'cha-cha'; and an onion squash with the gorgeous name of 'uchiki kuri'.

Corn ripe and ready for picking.

Top: pak choi.

Above: Tatsoi 'tah tsai'.

Opposite: Red cabbage 'rodynda'.

It is coldish but the sun is trying to peep through the grey and white clouds. But what a vast Norfolk sky! The countryside behind the cottage gently arcs and the sky seems to follow it round. 'I come out here of a morning,' says Peter, 'and I marvel at the hundreds of birds making their life here.' Prominent in the back field is a huge row of sunflowers which, even now past their prime, nonetheless are proving irresistible to small birds and tits hopping, pecking and flitting amongst them. This is evidently not anything to do with making money. 'No, my approach is not just to do with growing saleable things,' Peter explains. He points to the far end of the field, 'My beetle bank.'

'Beetle bank?'

'Sure. I see my role as working with nature to preserve and help the environment – the whole thing. Nature will provide if you 'go with it.' It has a wonderful system of checks and balances. There are beetle banks around each field – basically, a wide strip that we don't interfere with at all, so it is a haven for beetles. All sorts – we have the devil's coach horse beetle for one – and they need food so out they come and eat the predators which are mainly greenfly and aphids. Ladybirds and hoverflies also love aphids. Works brilliantly. We use absolutely no pesticides. The only thing we use is DiPel which is a biological pesticide: when the caterpillars feed on the brassica family – cabbages and so on – they ingest it and fall off. It is completely harmless to humans.'

We stop mid-field and look to where the crops grow in rough rows down towards the Church of St Mary. 'Rough' in the sense of having other things growing amongst them, too, sometimes. 'As long as my crops are healthy, I don't go bonkers weeding stuff out. These crops are happy.'

'Can crops be "happy"?' It is a silly townie question.

'Of course they can. A stressed crop will be weaker and more prone to attack from disease. As I said, you have to watch out for them.' Peter crouches down. 'Look at this. This is green kale. Next to it are the red and black varieties. Looking very happy!'

Suddenly, from across the far horizon, comes the sound of chopper blades as three helicopters arise a little incongruously into view. 'Apache gunships,' explains Peter. 'The Army Air Corp on exercises. You'll be safe as long as you don't try to run and hide among the trees and bushes!' He is teasing, of course, maybe enjoying this a bit. Nonetheless, Daniel and I decide to walk at a sedate pace behind him.

Peter knows a thing or two about the Armed Forces, having served for four years in the RAF. His job – aerospace systems operator – was based in one of the UK 'bunkers', tracking planes, talking to pilots and helping them protect the integrity of UK airspace. 'Fantastic job, and a great privilege.' I can well understand as my bro', Nigel, also served for twenty years in the RAF Regiment. I know what the service meant to him. 'It really sorted me out, says Peter, 'mixing with all different sorts of people. You can bring all that into business.'

We take a walk back to the lane and then up to the top field. I wonder if Peter has had any other jobs? 'Yes, I have. I have already said that when I was small I found the family emphasis on plants and stuff a bit too much. I rebelled a bit, I suppose. I went as a mature student to the UEA. Brilliant. Then I did a course on journalism.'

'Specialising in?'

'Sports. I loved competitive cycling. Do you have any particular sports love, Steve?'

'Sure do,' I reply. 'Cricket. I love it but was not much good at it. When I was at school, I was also for a time record holder at the 100 yards – not metres then – hurdles. Even now, my knees have some scars.'

'Daniel?' We are in the top field now.

'Not really. I was always very interested in drawing. I remember once, my Mum and Dad and me and sisters, Hannah and Laura, went to Norwich Cathedral. When I got home, I drew the Cathedral and my parents were amazed that I had somehow got the exact proportions of it into my head. Led to photography, I guess.'

It's getting a wee bit cold now. This top field contains wonderful specimens of tatsoi 'tah tsai' which looks like a large green rosette with spoon-shaped leaves. 'It's a Chinese vegetable and very good in winter. It is a form of pak choi. Try some.' Peter picks a leaf and hands it to Daniel and me. It has a wonderful succulent, peppery crunch. Next door is stem broccoli. 'You can eat it all, even the flowers,' he says. This one is sweeter, more delicate, nuttier.

There is a white covering over some of the crops. 'That's a spun web which we put over the crops. We do have a problem with pigeons, but that works just fine. It also creates a marvellous micro-climate where the crops can thrive.'

Opposite: January King cabbage 'Deadon'.

Below: Savoy cabbage 'Rigoletto'.

Bottom: Swiss chard.

Mustard Spinach 'Komatsuna'.

I spy some wonderful-looking carrot plants waving in the breeze. They are *huge*! I wonder how this is possible without pesticides as I have heard that carrot fly is a big problem. 'It is all to do with "knowing your enemy",' explains Peter. 'Timing is vital. We sow the carrots around the second week of June which is between the egg-laying periods.'

I ask Peter about soil. 'Soil is the basis of everything. This soil,' he indicates land to the north of where we are standing and where the Apache helicopters were, now thankfully gone, 'is very clay-like. The land to the south – over there, towards the church, is much more sandy and well-drained.'

'The best?'

'There is no best. You can do varying things with different soils. One of our biggest problems is the weather. We get terrible dry periods now – this spring we must have had 13 or 14 weeks without water. That can be devastating.'

'You have some amazing plants here,' says Daniel, crouching down to photograph some luscious-looking 'common' pak-choi. 'So what is a typical growing year?'

'Well, we start in the spring. First out of the ground are carrots and mixed salad leaves. Then, in the bean line we will start off with broad beans and early potatoes – varieties such as Rocket, Red Duke of York, Winston, Kestrel; and we grow Sante as a late second crop along with some salad potatoes. Then the first brassicas will be spring cabbage and calabrese – children will eat it if nothing else. Then purple-sprouting broccoli comes in March and finishes in late May, as well as the white-sprouting type which is always popular. Late May we will get all the salad things coming in, and beetroot, spring onions and we do a lot of kohl rabi. In the summer we grow courgettes, runner beans, and dwarf beans followed by peppers, tomatoes, and cucumbers. Some form of lettuce crop and rocket is grown throughout, and leeks, too. Following on in autumn comes sweetcorn, early squashes, cauliflowers – Italian cauliflower, Romanesco, is incredibly popular – black kale, red kale, green kale, and savoy cabbage. Then into sprouts, parsnips, swedes. Mid winter we harvest Jerusalem artichokes and leeks.'

I find it hard to imagine that there can be any time left for cycling, which we were talking about a few moments ago.

'Oh yes there is,' Peter replies. 'I cycle about 200 miles a week.'

'When on earth do you do that?' I ask, feeling that he must jump on to a parallel universe somewhere.

'When it is dark, mostly! It is the ideal release for me. People assume that as I work on the land, then that is enough. But, no, I need to disengage. I won prizes and things when I was younger. I love to cycle.'

'Oh, well,' I say, 'I guess that the land is flat around here. Tootling and so on.'

'No! Around here is too flat. I go to Essex where I can get some steeper terrain. I like a challenge. I am a hill rider.'

Peter with a box of produce ready to be dispatched to a customer.

CHASED BY TURKEYS BUT RUNNING AFTER GEESE

TURKEYS ARE NOT THE MOST intelligent of God's creatures. Decidedly dim, actually. 'You can put up a bit of silver paper in a tree, and they will look at it all day,' says Steve Childerhouse, owner of Great Grove Poultry in Attleborough, Norfolk.

But what magnificent creatures! Daniel kneels down to take a pic of a fine male Woodland Bronze. His beautiful bronze feathers shimmer in the sunshine while his striking but slightly bizarre red and blue head jerks back and forth in an arrogant, self important manner. The fleshy protuberance under the beak is called a wattle, whilst that hanging from his beak is known as a snood. He looks like he dates from the dawn of time – scientists think the 'modern' bird can be traced back at least a million years, which is much the same thing. At all events, he is king around here, strutting amongst hundreds of pure white hens. The din is indescribable. They have tiny little tufts for ears. If there is a brain in there it is surely scrambled by all the screeching.

They are very curious, though. As we wander through Great Grove's woodlands, hundreds of birds rush towards us, some from quite a long way off hurtling over in a comical side-to-side strut. Daniel is soon surrounded by a sea of white feathers and noise. These are the finest free range birds, left to wander at will in 35 acres of prime Norfolk woodland during the day with access to straw-filled barns at night. They will be processed when fully mature, which is between 24 and 27 weeks.

I wonder which sizes are most popular? 'The smaller ones, maybe 10 to 12 pounds, go quickly,' says Steve. 'Some, though, will grow to 35 pounds. As we don't use growth promoters or any kind of hormones, they are as individual as can be, so we don't always have the exact size every customer wants, but then I think they understand that when they come here.' And the diet? 'Cereals, mainly, and then, of course, they scratch around out here and find what they can.'

Opposite: Steve Childerhouse among his turkeys.

'This is how to carve a turkey!' Steve Childerhouse of Great Grove Poultry gives a demonstration in the Forum at Norwich during the Bidwells/EDP Food Festival.

Above: The breast of a turkey should be carved first. If it has been cooked breast-downward and only turned over for the final half hour or so in the oven to brown, the natural juices will remain in the meat.

Above right: A swirl of customers, some tasting, some asking questions and others just fascinated, surround Steve Childerhouse and Molly at the September Food Fair in Norwich.

Steve has always been keen on working on the farm. He was not always sure, though, exactly what direction his work would take. 'I used to have some chickens,' he says, 'but they were not really paying their way. So I decided to try rearing some turkeys.'

'How many did you start with?' I ask.

He smiles at the memory: 'four.'

'And how many have you got now?'

'Nine thousand. I'll maybe extend to twelve thousand, but that will be it. That's enough.'

I ask him if there was a critical time, maybe when he had to decide whether to expand to

Steve Childerhouse of Great Grove Turkeys has produced this exclusive recipe for our readers.

MEXICAN TURKEY

Ingredients:
1kg turkey breast/leg meat
1 can cream of chicken soup
1 (16 oz) sour cream
1 small can chopped green chilli's
1 tsp garlic salt
1lb White cheese
1lb Cheddar cheese (mild)
1 can chopped black olives
1 small pkg flour tortillas
1 can red enchilada sauce

Method:
Boil turkey 1 hour; remove skin and bone. Shred turkey. In medium bowl, mix soup, sour cream, chilli's, and garlic salt. Shred together both cheeses. Tear flour tortillas into thin strips. In 9 x 12 inch baking dish, layer ingredients like a lasagne: First ½ flour tortilla strips (cover bottom), ½ turkey, ½ soup mix, ½ olives, ½ cheese, 1/2 enchilada sauce; repeat layers. Bake at 350 degrees for 1 hour. Serve with hot sauce, sour cream and tortilla chips.

Can be frozen but freeze before baking.

Serving suggestion:
Hot sauce
Sour cream
Tortilla chips

Co-author, Daniel, surrounded by some fabulous Woodland Bronze birds: they are very curious and were quick to gather around.

such an extent, or perhaps get into other parts of farming? I am always amazed, when on a farm, at the 24/7 nature of the job, so I wonder also if he was ever tempted to work for Aviva maybe, or some other organisation where he could 'switch off' in the evenings and at weekends?

Steve laughs. 'Sure was. Both of those things. Also, it became clear at some point that I would need to invest a shedload of money if I was going to develop the business.'

'So what did you do?'

'Went trekking around Australia – good place to think things through!'

'Then?'

'Invested the required shedload.'

We are approaching the boundary with the road that leads up past the farmhouse to more acres of woodland. The turkeys are hot on our heels as we gingerly step over an electrified fence. Is this to keep the turkeys in?

'Sure, he says, 'and foxes out. Before we installed the electric fences we had some bad times. Once a fox got in and killed 13 – ate some but just left the rest. Some protection is virtually impossible, though. From the sky, for instance. One time a herring gull flew down and killed a few chicks. I must have hid in the hedge for six hours waiting for it to come down again but it didn't show. I went indoors for a cuppa and, blow-me-down, when I came out he had struck again. It's OK now because the birds are too big.'

As well as turkeys, Steve also keeps geese and it is them that we wander up the lane to see. In front of the farmhouse, however, is a piece of land around a pond. Grazing here is an old donkey and two fat-looking and complacent geese. 'Pets', explains Steve. 'As far as the goose and gander are concerned, well, they were about to be processed and the machinery broke down. They were the last two. So, we decided to keep them.'

It is a nice little story and I ask Steve what he has named them.

'Geese,' he replies, chuckling.

'I rule the roost around here!' A magnificent male Woodland Bronze turkey.

Full speed ahead! Turkeys will rush and strut towards you in an amusing fashion.

Opposite: Watching Wimbledon! Unlike turkeys, geese are less inquisitive and will flock in a tight group, their heads following any movement in unison. This can sometimes give a comic effect as if they are watching a tennis match.

We are accompanied now by two border collies, Flo and Meg. It strikes me that they must have the best life possible. 'Yeah! They love it. Meg is a rescue dog, very nervous when we got her but now she likes nothing better than rounding up the turkeys and geese.' As we go into another open barn which serves as the night quarters for the bronze turkeys Meg comes in with us and crouching low, every sinew alert and eyes a-quiver, guards the exit. We have come here to see the feeding stations. 'They contain high-nutrient cereal pellets,' Steve informs us. All around is hay, with some square bales piled up, turkeys on every horizontal surface. It looks comical, almost as if they are holding a meeting straight out of Orwell's *Animal Farm*.

Stepping up the lane a little farther and crossing some newly-planted woodland, we come across hundreds of geese. Stouter, and with a noticeably lower centre of gravity, they seem to be playing in a field of mud. 'They created that themselves,' says Steve. 'They are incredibly mucky.'

Talking turkey. Co-author, Stephen (L) and owner of Great Grove Poultry, Steve Childerhouse (R) get down to the finer points of turkey-rearing, in front of some Woodland Bronze birds.

They are also very different in personality from the turkeys. As we approach the field, they turn tail and run. Daniel has to chase them around to get a pic or two. 'They are much more intelligent than the turkeys.' Steve looks pensive. 'Sometimes I am convinced they know what is coming.'

Geese, in Victorian times the bird of choice for Christmas before being largely supplanted by the turkey, is making a big comeback. This is maybe because English cooking is now much more adventurous than it once was. Gone are the days – not too long ago – when it could be truly said, as some guide books did, 'to eat well in England you must have breakfast three times a day.'

And what is on the menu at Great Grove Poultry on Christmas Day – goose or turkey? 'Turkey at Christmas,' laughs Steve, 'and Goose for New Year!'

We go back to the farmhouse for a welcome cup of tea. I take the chance to ask Steve about the best way to cook a turkey. 'Breast down', he says, 'and then, about thirty minutes before the end of cooking, carefully turn the bird around so that the breast can brown. The number one rule is not to overcook it. If you do that – and lots of people do – you ruin all our hard work.'

'And what about stuffing the inside - my Mum always used to put chestnut stuffing into the cavity.' I mention. Would he recommend that?

'No, I wouldn't actually, although a lot of people like to cook it this way as it adds flavour. But I think it interferes with the uniform cooking of the bird, so I would recommend putting a peeled onion or large Bramley apple inside instead.'

And how does he explain the current interest in fine food in the UK? 'Well, we've come a long way, haven't we? There are TV chefs galore. But it probably really all started around here with our very own Delia Smith.' And his particular favourites? 'Take a look at this,' he smiles. 'We send thousands of these recipe leaflets out: 'Turkey and Creamy Stilton Pies', now they're really great, or 'Turkey, Bacon and Sweetcorn Chowder' – that is a brilliant way to use up leftover turkey.' His favourite? 'Oh, I don't know, I love them all. But I have a special place in my heart for a recipe we have adapted ourselves – 'Crunchy Peanut Butter Turkey and Coconut Curry with Coriander'. Here is the recipe:

CRUNCHY PEANUT BUTTER TURKEY AND COCONUT CURRY WITH CORIANDER

Ingredients:
1 large onion, peeled and roughly chopped
2 cloves garlic, peeled
2 tbsp rapeseed oil
2 tbsp balti paste
1 tbsp tomato puree
1 tbsp cumin
2 tbsp crunchy peanut butter
1 14ox can chopped tomatoes
1 14oz can coconut milk
Juice of 1 lime
3 tbsp fresh coriander
1 tbsp sultanas
8 fl oz turkey stock
24 oz cooked Totally Traditional Turkey, cut into chunks

Method:
Put the onion and garlic in a processor and chop until almost mushy. In a wok or deep sauté pan, heat the oil and fry the onion mixture until it starts to brown, then stir in the balti paste, tomato puree and cumin and fry for a further minute.

Stir in the peanut butter and fry on a low heat until the oil begins to separate and the sauce has darkened.

Add the tomatoes, coconut milk, lime juice, 2 teaspoons of coriander, sultanas and stock and gently simmer for about twenty minutes. Add the cooked turkey and simmer for five minutes or until hot and heated through.

Serve with rice, thick yogurt and sprinkle with the remaining teaspoon of coriander.

It is obviously a cue to go home and have some dinner. It has been a great day. We drive slowly away. We are only a few miles out of Norwich but the air smells so fresh and as far as we can see – for miles – the flattish fields are differing shades of green or a freshly tilled deep brown. I find myself muttering 'Different world, isn't it? Different world.'

OFF TO MARKET

MARKETS ARE VERY FAMILIAR territory to Daniel who is often at craft fairs and markets of various sorts himself, selling his photographic work and books. He has got to know many of the specialist food producers over the years – in fact, this book includes the wonderful pickles, jams and chutneys of Liz Joint with whom he has shared many a happy market day.

Farmers' Markets are perhaps the best known way to buy fresh, organic Norfolk produce, though by no account the only means – Farm Shops are also excellent, and we highlight Norton's Shop in the section on Dairy Farming. You can also grow your own or, increasingly, find a surprising variety of good Norfolk food in supermarkets. About both of which, a little more later.

Back to Farmers' Markets: there are now lots of them as they have boomed in recent years. They are not on in every place in every week – maybe the second Saturday of each month or something like that – but, if you are around during weekends at any of the following Norfolk locations, do check with your local council info office or Library to see what's going on.

There are pork pies, and then there are Norfolk pork pies!

Aylsham Farmers' Market, early morning.

Opposite: Stephen is fascinated by some local cheese at a Farmers' Market.

67

SOME NORFOLK FARMERS' MARKETS

Acle, Aylsham, Banham, Beccles, Blakeney, Burston, Creake Abbey, Dereham Railway Station, Dersingham, Diss Market Place, Fakenham, Fritton Lake, Harleston, Holt, Lophams Village Hall, Marham, Metfield, Neatisland, North Runcton, Norwich – Gentleman's Walk, Golden Triangle, Earlham House, Norfolk Showground, Bastwick, Rushall, Sandringham, Snettisham, Spixworth, Stalham, Stradbroke, Swaffham, Thorpe St Andrew, Watton, Wroxham and Wymondham. A new departure is the Norfolk and Suffolk local food website www.welovelocalfood.co.uk

They are all interesting for various reasons. Stradbroke, for instance, is run by senior school students as part of a business studies course; Gentleman's Walk in Norwich hosts a friendly invasion of French traders periodically selling all sorts of edible continental treats; some specialise in famous Norfolk seafood, some maybe in venison or the finest Aberdeen Angus beef and some also sell arts and crafts. Locals seem to have a thing about pork pies and sausages in particular – you will nowhere find better. And, of course, you can buy, often trying first, everything from honey to ducks eggs to goats' cheeses (they go down wonderfully well with a local ale from one of the burgeoning number of micro-brewers in Norfolk and Suffolk, who are also on hand to slake your thirst after a hard day's 'slog' around all the market stalls).

The weather may leave a lot to be desired but Aylsham Market soon becomes very busy

Clockwise from top left: Mrs Temple's Cheese is well-known throughout the county; Binham Blue; Free range eggs are a common find at farmers markets and farm shops; Chillis Galore is a well-known maker of chilli-based sauces and jellies and can often be seen at Norfolk Farmers' Markets.

The freshest seasonal food

Most noted products, maybe, are the fresh local fruits and veggies, possibly picked an hour or so before you buy. Norfolk soils range from light and sandy to heavy-as-can-be and the weather is as diverse – infuriatingly sometimes – as anywhere in the UK, with the result that the array and quality of vegetables and fruit is incomparable. The local markets reflect the seasons as one would expect and the following is a brief description of what will be available at different times of the year.

WINTER

Root vegetables such as turnips, swede, parsnips, beetroot, cabbage, cauliflower, brussel sprouts (sweet, not bitter as I remember from school!), potatoes, celeriac, red, green and purple kale and leeks

Above and opposite: Pumpkins are fun for carving but also deliciously sweet.

SPRING

Rhubarb (superb on its own or for jellies and pies), asparagus, spinach, cucumber, radishes and spring onions

SUMMER

We really get going here: all sorts of salad leaf, beans – green, broad and melt-in-the-mouth runners, broccoli, new Norfolk potatoes and the sometimes overlooked fine local garlic. This is also fruit time – blueberries, greengages, blackcurrants, strawberries, wild raspberries and (very fat and succulent) strawberries

AUTUMN

Blackberries, apples, plums, pears, sloes, elderberries, damsons and quince; vegetables include mushrooms, leeks, carrots, lettuce and marrow and, of course, pumpkins and marrows

About Apples – an overdue celebration?

Norfolk is famous for many foods – sugar, turkeys and mustard probably spring most readily to mind. To the co-authors of this book, this seems a little unfair as it was the apple that, as much as anything, brought great fame to our county in days gone by. This is perhaps surprising because Suffolk, Kent and other counties grew the best known varieties before medieval times. Nonetheless, by Tudor times, Norwich was famously described as 'a city in an orchard or an orchard in a city' so many were the trees to be seen everywhere. Such are the perceived health-giving properties of an apple – I was surprised to discover that the pips contain cyanide actually, though not anywhere near enough to cause any harm – and that today the young ladies of Norwich, aged mid-twenties to mid-thirties, hold the UK record for the number of apples eaten, which is one a day.

Apples – and pears to a lesser extent – were used to make cider which, since medieval times, has been a form of Norfolk currency. Landowners would accept rent in this form and the gentry would send barrels to the monarch in lieu of taxes. Up until almost the end of the 20th century Norfolk was pre-eminent in cider production, both apple and pear based; the huge Gaymers factory in Attleborough sadly closing its doors for the final time in 1995. The decline in the Norfolk apple industry has been catastrophic: A Norfolk Orchards Survey of 2006 found that orchards in Norfolk reduced by 85 % after 1950 and by a further third in the early years of the present century.

Lost and found

Some wonderful varieties have been lost over the years. And yet, have they? A fascinating story was reported in the national press in 2009 when a retired GP, Kevin Browne, aged 80, rediscovered the 'extinct' Norfolk Dumpling apple, a pale yellow/greenish cooker, in a

Home grown Cox apples.

Bramley apples.

walled garden he had purchased in North Creake. There are about 30 or 40 others as I have discovered, too, which have not been seen for a while but may exist somewhere. They have the most marvellous names. Here are a few:

• Belle Grideline, a yellow and red Norwich apple not heard of since 1884

• Ten Shilling Apple, a green dessert apple not heard of since 1934

• Bland's Jubilee, a perfumed, conical apple with large russet spots, created by Norwich grower, Michael Bland, just after 1800. Not heard of since 1884

• Norwich Jubilee. Medium sized apple not heard of since 1872

• Norfolk/Winter Coleman. Dating from the first half of the 18th century in Aylsham, this ribbed carmine-coloured apple has not been heard of since 1884

• Early Nonpareil. An aromatic and juicy yellow apple propagated by Mr Stagg of Caister-on-Sea, late 18th century. Not heard of since the 1920s

• Colonel Harbord's Pippin. This was first grown not long after the Battle of Waterloo at Gunton Hall, near Cromer. A very attractive fruit part greenish yellow and part reddy brown, it is only relatively recently 'lost', in the 1970s in fact, so Colonel Harbord's pride and joy more than likely still exists in somebody's back garden

Good to relate, there are still over 40 varieties grown and thriving to a greater or lesser degree, some here and some there, all over Norfolk. Local Farmers' Markets and Farmers' Shops are a treasure trove of local types. It can be great fun to try to spot a name that you, or the children, have not seen before. Here are just a few you might see: Happisburgh; Norfolk Royal; Five Crowned Pippin – if you spot this one, give yourself a special treat as it is probably the oldest surviving variety, maybe from the 1300s; Lynn's Pippin (Lynn is the name of the grower and it is actually from Emneth); Caroline - from Blickling Hall and named after Lord Suffield's wife; St Magdalen, from Downham Market; Sandringham, raised at Sandringham House late 19th century; Harling Hero, from East Harling; Green Roland, also known as Norfolk Green Queen, from about 1800; Emneth Early, another William Lynn creation; Norfolk Royal Russet, sweet, chewy with hints of pear, and many people's favourite; and Vicar of Beighton, named after the rectory in that parish and propagated by the Revd Fellows.

NORFOLK APPLE AND MIXED FRUIT BREAD

In bygone days, no apples would be deliberately wasted unlike, alas, today when many are just left to rot as it is 'uneconomic' in monetary terms to do anything with them. Partly, this is because the old country knowledge has been lost – some are good for keeping in a dark space for Christmas apple pies and some aren't, a few varieties make good juice, some cook-up well, a few have just the right 'bite' and flavour for chutneys, some with good flavours make excellent home-made wine (I can heartily recommend my recipe for Norfolk apple and blackcurrant home-made wine providing you don't aim, after sampling it, to go to work next day) and so on. Well, the joy of the following recipe is that you can use pretty much any apples you happen to have around, adjusting the spices and fruit according to how much flavour you want. It is also very simple. I give the quantities in the recipe itself.

Ingredients:
4/5 Norfolk apples
Mixed Fruit, or any plums, cherries or pears you have in the kitchen
Self-Raising flour
Brown sugar is best but white or golden will do
Butter or margarine
1 beaten egg
Cinnamon/Nutmeg
Mixed spice
Dessicated coconut if you like

Method:
Wash and chop apples. Put in bowl and add about half as much mixed fruit.

In another bowl put about half the total above volume of self-raising flour. Mix in half a pack of butter and other ingredients.

Mix both bowls together. The mixture should be creamy. If not, add more butter or some milk or some of both.

Put in a greased tin and in the oven at about 180 degrees centigrade for about half an hour.

Serve warm with Norfolk Dairy Farm buttermilk or cream. Or leave until cold and slice as a cake.

It is worth mentioning cherries, too, as you will see many many varieties in Farmers' Markets, all in summer and all of very recent introduction. Norfolk is very fortunate in having the John Innes Research Institute at Colney which is actively developing canker-free strains. Some you may see are Merpet, prolific and black-skinned; Mermat, a large variety with red flesh; Pat, medium black skinned; Inge, large and a prolific grower; and Hertford, which has a dark red skin.

We mustn't forget bread – the best, to my mind, comes fresh to market from artisan bakers like Pye Bakers of Norwich, featured in this book. You must get there quickly, however, as it goes quick as a flash!

Growing your own

Part of the 'back to good food' movement is the demand for allotments. In the Norwich area at the moment there is a waiting list of about 500 people. If you want one, you have to put your name down. Daniel's Dad and himself got one last year and Daniel says, the back-breaking task of getting it ready apart, 'there is nothing to compare with lifting our own potatoes or carrots for Sunday lunch!'

How should you prepare your allotment? I would suggest digging and weeding – dandelions and dock make fearsome foes! It is a good idea to test the pH value of the soil to see which nutrients are lacking. Some Norfolk soil is light and sandy, in which case add potash and phosphates in the form of organic matter and natural fertiliser. This will also help 'bulk it up'. If it is wet and clay-like, it is harder work to dig but it will be higher in natural nutrients and maybe just some nitrogen will suffice. Be careful not to overfeed, though, as this will result in your crops going a bit bonkers and stringy which in turn will encourage pests.

Easy crops to begin with are potatoes, runner beans, tomatoes, beetroot and leeks. Early spring is best time to sow seeds or, if using seedlings from a nursery, wait a little until the worst of the cold snaps have gone. Herbs – rosemary, sage, thyme in particular – are very easy to grow, too.

In various parts of this book we talk about 'natural' pest control – well, in an allotment, I would recommend also growing some annual flowers as these will attract pests away from the veg and also look lovely on the kitchen windowsill.

I was interested to find out during the research for this chapter that allotments are largely

Opposite: Beetroot can be a very rewarding crop for first-time allotment holders.

A bursting pod of Norfolk peas,
succulent and sweet.

Home-grown tomatoes maturing at
different times on the same plant.

the result of the Victorian crusade against drink, seen as the curse of the working man – or, more accurately in some cases as the problem was so bad, it was the case of work being the curse of the drinking man. As we say in our book *Norwich* (Halsgrove Discover Series) it is not an exaggeration to say that, for many of our forefathers, leisure was spent either drinking or building a church, though hopefully not at the same time. It was thought that an allotment would give the working man something better to do than go down the accursed pub. Naturally, the 'Dig for Victory' campaign in the last war saw a huge increase in the number of allotments and today the demand is peaking again due to the drive for good food. Theoretically the local council has to provide enough to meet demand, although this seems a tad unrealistic these days with land fetching huge prices.

Rods, oxen and cricket pitches

I have, incidentally, also learned a few things about measurements and allotments. The standard size is 10 rods, a rod being the length of the rod needed to control a team of eight oxen in the days of our forefathers, which is 5.5 yards. A chain is four rods which is the exact and correct length of a cricket wicket. Just to round things off, a furlong is 10 chains and 8 furlongs make a mile. It is, I think, understandable why so many proud Norfolk citizens refuse to throw away such fabulously-arrived-at and ancient calculations for the EU's matter-of-fact and bland metres and centimetres!

Supermarkets

All is not lost, either, on the supermarket front. Such famous local names as Bakers and Larners of Holt, East of England Co-op and Roys of Wroxham are sourcing local produce where possible, the latter selling honey from Orchid Apiaries which we feature in this book. Marks & Spencer stock Cromer crabs, which we also feature, and the bigger supermarket chains are responding to pressure from the public to give local produce space and to cut down on 'air miles'. If we keep buying it, they will keep stocking it, I guess.

There is really nothing to compare with digging up your own carrots for Sunday lunch!

WONDERFUL NORFOLK PICKLES, PRESERVES, JAMS AND CORDIALS

EBENEZER COTTAGE IS A lovely pink thatched cottage, dating from 1601, tucked away in the Norfolk village of Bunwell. As Daniel carefully manoeuvres the car down the crunchy gravel track towards the front of the cottage, a slight figure with a huge smile comes out to greet us. This is Liz Joint, rapidly gaining an enviable reputation for the finest pickles, preserves and cordials in the county, and it is the lady we have come to see.

As Liz guides us towards the open back door a lovely, fruity and rich aroma drifts out towards us. It is coming, as we soon realise, from a cauldron of gooseberries cooking on the stove, quietly emitting a regular splitter and splutter. 'For my gooseberry jam,' says Liz. 'My Grandmother's recipe.'

Opposite: Succulent jellies from local produce in Liz's kitchen.

Ebenezer Cottage dates from 1601.

'Welcome to my kitchen!'
Liz Joint at work in
Ebenezer Cottage.

The kitchen in which we are standing overlooks uninterrupted Norfolk countryside, beyond the grape vines, blackcurrant bushes and trees heavy with crab apples. 'I grow everything I can,' says Liz, seeing where our eyes are wandering. 'If I can't, then I go to my favourite farm shop in Mulbarton - you know, where you can be sure that the pears, onions or pumpkins are really grown on site - not imported.' She breaks into a loud chuckle. 'Now Daniel, what do you want to photograph?'

Daniel goes for the cauldron of gooseberries. I look around the kitchen, a small one for so much produce – there are jars everywhere, some with their tops on, some with them off, cooling, and others complete with a label and Liz's trademark blue-and-white gingham tops tied round with string, waiting to be sent off to shops. Liz directs me to a table on which she has placed some lovely crumbly cheese and an open jar of translucent amber jelly.

'Have you ever had Norfolk cheese and homemade crab apple jelly? Not many people,' she says, 'think of fine cheese and jelly. I have never been much of a sweet dessert person, more of a cheese person. You should not adulterate such produce with bread or crackers.' I taste it: incredible – tangy and clean, sweet and piquant, all at the same time.

'Ha!' she says. 'Now try this – one of my favourite products, blackberry cordial. I made this a few years ago for my friends. I sent it to them for Christmas.' Liz produces a small glass and pours some deep purple liquid, almost glugging, into it. 'Nowadays I only make it for my family and friends as I could never keep up with large scale production. Go on, Steve, try it – what do you think?'

'It's just so… so… *strong and blackberry - y*, Liz,' I blurt out with watering eyes. 'Fabulous!'

Daniel is still at the cauldron. 'That must be your 20th shot,' I say. 'What is this, 'The Book of Gorgeous Gooseberries?'

'You know what I am like, Steve!'

Liz raises a questioning eyebrow. I explain. 'He won't let up until he has the absolutely perfect shot. Our recent book, *The Spirit of Norwich Cathedral*, has about 65 pics. How many did you take for that?'

'About 800, I think,' Daniel replies with a wide grin. 'Not that I minded at all!'

I am curious as to how Liz came to start this fascinating business. Family background, maybe? 'Not really,' says Liz, 'I actually spent 26 years with Norwich Union. Very happy ones. But after a merger or two I found my particular field of expertise was based in York. Well, what with all the travelling and living out of a suitcase, moving back and forth, I found I was becoming exhausted. So when I actually came home, I would spend the time getting rid of the grime and city life just walking about this area, getting some fresh air and chilling out a bit. It was during these walks that I was amazed to find so much natural, 'free' food – the wonderful Norfolk crab apples were the first things I noticed. Then the blackberries, rosehips and sloes - so it went on.'

'Even so,' I remark, 'it must have been a bit of a leap to actually give up a well paid job in order to start a fledgling business?'

Below: In Liz's kitchen. The Norfolk apple industry has suffered a disastrous decline since 1950, but many varieties are now being rediscovered as discussed in these pages.

Bottom: A corner of Liz's kitchen showing produce ready for market.

'Not really, Steve. I was in love, you see, with Norfolk and all the wonderful crops and foods around us here. If anything, my time away made me long for it more. Ever been in love?'

'Possibly, but that's a bit classified…' I think I turn red.

'Yes you have, I can tell. That's something else we Norfolk folk are good at – seeing things!' Liz gives one of her, now rapidly becoming' trademark' chuckles.

Moving on quickly, I ask 'How did it go? Did your friends think you were bonkers?'

Opposite: 'The finest gooseberries doth the best preserve make'.

A cauldron of gooseberries cooking on the stove.

Daniel has now finally moved his camera away from the gooseberries and is busy sizing up the jars of pickled eggs.

'No, they were all fully supportive and I am very happy that I started selling the produce straight away – craft fairs, local farm shops and so on.'

'OK, but where do you get your recipes from?'

'Some came from my Grandma. She was a wonderful cook, so maybe it is a bit in the genes. Mind you, she was such a good cook that she never gave quantities, which is very frustrating as I have to do a great deal of experimenting to make them work today! Others come from old Norfolk cookbooks.'

Ebenezer Cottage garden: ripe apples fresh on the tree, waiting to be picked.

'I remember my grandfather having a huge vegetable plot and my grandmother cooking with all the vegetables and fruit he grew. Even after my grandmother died, my grandfather (in his seventies) made his own piccalilli from his own grown vegetables. I have a few very precious cookbooks from my grandmother which I treasure and have used as reference for all my produce and my prize possession is the old crock pot she used for pigeon casserole. However at school I was a disaster at domestic science (as it was called in those days) and remember clearly the day I had to go home from school and tell my parents they needed to pay the school for three pudding basins that I had managed to break in one lesson!'

'So what are your main products now?' I ask. Daniel is looking strangely at the pickled eggs.

'I do chutneys, pickles, jams, jellies, marmalades and cordials. I have also started to make a county mustard and some flavoured salts.' And Liz's favourite? 'I have two. The crab apple jelly, which you have tasted, is one. The other is a garden mint cordial. It is simply fantastic mixed with sparkling water. Very refreshing.'

Liz has created a brand new chutney for this book. 'My local butcher has been on to me for ages to make a new chutney. A bit hot though not enough to blow your head off.' We have decided to call it 'Ebenezer Chutney', after her lovely cottage. I remark that, as Charles Dickens' greatest fan, I am delighted to create something in his name. 'Ah,' says Liz, laughing, 'but my cottage name is not to do with that great man: it is named after the Ebenezer religion which thrived around here some time ago.'

EBENEZER CHUTNEY

Ingredients:

1 teaspoon dried chilli flakes (or 2 fresh red chillies deseeded and finely chopped)
10 large cooking apples (chopped)
1 clove garlic (crushed)
375g Raisins
115g Glace Ginger (chopped)
1kg Brown Sugar
1 litre Vinegar
1 tbsp salt
1 tsp mixed spice
2 tsp Chinese five spice
1 tbsp ground turmeric
2 bay leaves

Instructions:

1 Place all ingredients into a preserving pan.
2 Stir over heat and bring to the boil.
3 Reduce heat and simmer uncovered for approx 2hrs (or until mixture thickens).
4 Remove bay leaves
5 Spoon mixture into sterilised jars and seal while hot

Fresh chillies for
Ebenezer Chutney.

'And the pickled eggs?' Daniel breaks in. 'They don't really seem to go with all your other produce.'

'Ah, yes, I thought you might query that,' laughs Liz. 'Well, we started to keep chickens and I found I regularly had a glut of eggs. So I pickled then down. It seems a strange thing for Norfolk but my local butcher cannot get enough and, as he says, you cannot get fresher.'

Liz asks: 'Would you like to see round my garden?' Wouldn't we just! We go outside – it is mid-afternoon and the weather is not all that great, but this part of Norfolk has a soft touch, a friendly dampness. I recall Peter Ackroyd's fantastic biography of London where he

Grapes on the vine in the cottage garden.

describes a wet London as like seeing humanity through a veil of tears. Not so here: there is something pure, untrammelled and primeval about a Norfolk wet afternoon. It is almost as if the rain particles hold back a little, not wanting to land on you with anything but the gentlest of force.

We see eating apples, rowan berries, crab apples, pears, rhubarb and onions. And chickens.

Raucous shrieks from a nest of crows rents the air. 'Don't get too comfortable,' they seem to be saying. 'This is Norfolk.'

Rowan berries.

BORN INTO IT. IT'S A LIFE

SAT NAVS ARE A GREAT HELP most of the time. Not, unfortunately, always. Ask the lady who was blithely driving along a country road in Somerset one wet and cold night recently, relying on her sat nav, and ended up slowly sinking into a bog. Or a friend of mine in Norwich whose flat was built over an archway leading to a small 'quad' of houses. He was watching England lose to Portugal one evening on TV when 'thwack!' a delivery truck ploughed into his flat: the driver had been following instructions and neither he, nor the sat nav, realised that there was a flat built over the roadway.

Daniel and I had been enjoying a pleasant drive along twisty Norfolk roads on the way to Norton's Farm Shop and Dairy in Frettenham when we turned into a small cul-de-sac of immaculate detached bungalows. 'You have arrived at your destination', intoned the machine in a friendly feminine voice.

'Look like a farm to you, Steve?' asked Daniel.

'Well, er, no, not a lot….'

We hurriedly abandoned the thing and, checking a map on the mobile phone, drove another couple of miles until we saw the sign for 'Norton's Farm Shop' to our right, down a long country track. We turned the machine on again for fun. 'Recalculating,' it said. 'Reverse, and proceed two point eight miles…' The shop came into sight.

'Oh, shut up,' we both said in unison, and pulled out the lead.

The shop is quite a large single-storey building situated, it has to be said, a little way from the 'main' road. Inside, though, it is an Aladdin's cave of fine Norfolk produce – fresh vegetables, ice cream, cakes, local meats and, of course, Norton's own milk, creams and

Opposite: Everything from fresh Norton's milk and butter, to fresh veggies, to ice-cream, jams and cakes is there to tempt you in Rona's shop.

Above: Rona and some of her milk, buttermilk and butter.

Above right: 'But Rona, this cabbage is so *green*…' says Daniel.

butters. When we enter, Rona Norton, who runs the business as part of the larger Norton family firm - which includes an agricultural and a dairy farm – is serving Nicky Powles, a local resident who has lived about 100 yards up the road for the last ten years, and before that wasn't far away either, being pure Norfolk through and through. I ask Nicky what she is buying.

'Lots of veggies, cream and some pork. Don't need milk as Rona delivered some last night.'

'Deliveries? I thought no-one delivered milk anymore.'

'Ah, I do!' says Rona. 'I have a round of about sixty houses in the village. And I deliver in the evening because one reason the delivery system stopped was that people did not want milk left on the doorstep all day when they were out at work.'

'What kind of hours do you work, then?' asks Daniel, setting up his photo equipment in front of some succulent-looking leeks, squashes and cabbages. 'Must be a colossal amount. By the way, this cabbage is just so… *green*!'

'Oh, I don't count hours.' Rona gives a ready laugh. 'I am a farmer's wife – I just get on with it. And the cabbage, yes, it has just come from the fields, about half an hour ago.'

'I'll take one of those, too,' says Nicky, picking up a cabbage. 'About milk - I have horses and like to ride around looking at the cattle in the fields – then in the evening I get to drink their milk. It's brilliant!'

Daniel and I have arranged to visit Norton's Farm shop and to meet Rona and Philip, her husband. Philip will take us around the dairy farm in a little while. There are two farms, Beck Farm and Church Farm, the former basically arable and the latter a mix of arable and grass.

'By the way, you two were a little late,' laughs Rona. 'Got to keep to time on a farm, so much to get on with!'

'Ah, yes, we had a little trouble with the sat nav…'

'Let me guess, it deposited you a couple of miles away up a cul-de-sac – it's always doing that.' We laugh and she explains. 'Sometimes I get calls from customers and have to guide them here on their mobiles. Must be something to do with the terrain, or the RAF or… goodness knows what…' Rona breaks into yet another laugh and it is impossible not to join in: good produce and good humour seem to go together in these parts.

Rona makes us coffee while explaining future expansion plans for the shop. 'It is a little bit down a side track but more and more people are finding us.' To emphasise the point, another lady customer comes in. She and Rona obviously know one another well as they exchange a friendly 'Morning!'. 'Yes, we will soon have a café and the shop itself will be extended.'

Rona introduces Daniel and me to the lady, now at the counter. 'Hi there, I am Noami, Naomi Linder - live just up the road.' We ask Noami why she shops here. 'I'm local Frettenham and I like to buy local. It is good to know where food comes from and it also hasn't travelled miles and miles. It's also obviously good for local business.'

I remember reading somewhere that for every £10 spent in a local village or farm shop a total of £24 is created within the local economy – much more than if you shop in a supermarket.

A van pulls up and offloads some milk, buttermilk and cream – Norton's, of course. 'From our own Dairy,' says Rona. I think it must be nice to have a delivery from yourself.

'Ah, Emily.' A young lady enters and is introduced as one of Rona's daughters. 'Emily is very interested in the farms. She has just been to a neighbour's pig farm – 'did you buy one, then?'

'No,' replies Emily, 'I bought four. I didn't really mean to. I was going to go for a really cute one with black markings but she wouldn't get in the trailer. Her three mates got in uninvited, though and by the time we got her on board they all seemed so well acquainted it seemed a shame to split them up.'

The phone rings. It is Philip. 'He's back now from the fields – let me take you up to the house.' The house is only a few yards from the shop and we are soon sitting around the farmhouse table with cups of tea.

Philip looks lithe and fit, and speaks with a decided Norfolk lilt, neither of which is surprising seeing he is a farmer and was born and brought up on the farm. 'My father, Jack, bought Church Farm in 1946 and this one in 1961.'

'Have the farms changed much?' I ask.

'Well, originally Church Farm was a mixed farm. Always had some dairy cows, though – at one time my father had a Pedigree Shorthorn herd and later we had Friesians. You will have to ask my nephew, David, any of the finer points…'

'Why's that?'

'We run the farm as a partnership, you see. David looks after the dairy side of things and I take care of the arable side. It's very good to have a family partnership as we can both help to keep the Norton name and business for the next generation. Emily's interested in coming in to the farm in a big way soon, which is good.'

Opposite: Take your pick of the finest veggies!

I explain that we have just met Emily in the Farm Shop. 'She's bought some pigs.'

'Has she now?' Philip laughs. 'Well, I'm not surprised!'

I wonder who is the accountant in the business – who, for example says when it is OK to go out and buy pigs, tractors or other things?

'Oh, that is Rona. She did a business studies course. She will say 'Go and buy a trailer or tractor now, or something.'

I ask Philip to talk about his special responsibility – the agricultural side of the farm. What, for example, does he grow? 'First of all, food for the cattle. That's grass, most importantly. At Church Farm we have about 60 acres where we sow grass in 5 year leys – grass for five years, maybe, and then it is ploughed up for 2-3 years of an arable crop. We grow some forage maize – corn to Americans – which we cut at the end of September. Makes good silage.'

'You make all your own silage?' I explain that we have recently been to see Jane Cargill at Foxley Wood Farm and she was telling us how she made the silage for her Angus Aberdeen herd.

'Oh Jane, yes, Rona knows her – went on a college course together!' I am beginning to realise what an interconnected world Norfolk farming is.

Silage must be very important, then? 'Sure, we need it for feed all the year round. It fills the belly.'

Philip also devotes about 25 hectares to sugarbeet, some of which is used for the dairy herd, along with winter barley and wheat.

Soil is the basis of everything, he explains. 'Good soil will be undamaged by machinery, there will be no compaction and it will be free draining.'

'On one of our trips,' remembers Daniel, 'we spent a day with Peter Burgess who grows 65 different kinds of veggies in Sisland, and he was telling us that there is not really 'best' soil – you just do what you can with what you have. Would you agree with that?'

'Absolutely. Although as a rule stony soil is a bit of a nuisance. But, yes, different soils need treating separately. Crops on light soil are prone to scorching - a lot of Beck Farm land is very light land so we put lots of muck into it - fortunately, we have a lot of that! Then you are careful what you grow on it: we grow a fair bit of spring barley as it has a short season. Rabbits are a problem around here – lots of old quarries hereabouts – and we get the crop up before they get into it! We'll grow some maize as well.'

And on the heavier soil? 'Sugarbeet and potatoes, maybe, although it's best to plant potatoes on land with as few stones as possible.'

Are there any rules passed on from generation to generation? 'Yeah, about your working day – "work as if it is the last day like that", which means firstly, don't put things off till tomorrow cos' that day will likely be completely different. And then make the most of the weather … If it is wet, do 'wet' things and if it's dry…' He leaves the sentence to finish itself.

Philip at work.

As always, when on a farm, I am awed by the amount of time needed to run the place efficiently, to say nothing of the commitment of the men and women involved. 'So, Philip,' I begin, a little mischievously perhaps, 'do you ever wish you had gone to work in a nice 9–5 job, clean office, lots of coffee, company car, weekends off...?' I know already what he is going to say by the look on Philip's face.

'Absolutely never!' He laughs out loud. 'Steve, Daniel, look out that window – I can walk 100 metres, whatever, here and there and I know that this is *our* land – not mine, maybe, as I am one of a partnership keeping it for the next generation. You see, you have to be born into it to realise it is not just to do with having a job. It is a life. A business, too, sure, but *much* more than that...'

'A rich life?' I ask with a big grin.

Philip forks silage to the herd.

'Not in money terms, but in terms of a full life and satisfaction and stuff like that, well that is something else.'

We have finished our tea. 'I expect you would like to see the herd?' Philip asks. We would, very much. 'Follow me in your car, then. The dairy farm is just the other side of the village.'

A few minutes later we draw up outside a huge cattle shed and step outside. It is very muddy. No wellies. It's got to be a case of rolling trousers up and hosing down the shoes later. The air smells of a mixture of cow and hay which is quite potent. There are lots of 'moos' as the herd has sensed our arrival.

'They're inside now, of course,' Philip says, 'but they are outside as long as possible. They even take a "holiday" – we have 30 acres of marshland and we put them out there once a year for the month or two before they are due to calve while they are not being milked.'

At the front of the cattle shed is the milking area. Up top are the temporary pens, herringbone fashion, where the cows are held for milking. They are milked 12 at a time. Down below is a dug-out portion where humans work. Milking is twice a day, about 5.30-ish in the morning and 3.30 in the afternoon. The farm may move into 'robot' milking one day but this will involve important logistical questions – like where do you put the milking station in relation to the cows and it is also likely to cost a six figure sum just to buy the basics.

'It's a big family exercise as it is,' Philip explains, 'to get all the milking done, clean out the shed while the cows are being milked, keep the place clean and so on,' He points to a small building just behind us. 'The last couple of years, we've done our own bottling, too.' I mention that we were in the shop when there was a delivery of milk. 'Yep', he says, 'that's where it came from.'

We pass into the sheds. The Moo Symphony increases. Heads of beautiful heifers lean out from the railings which keep them in their extensive living areas. I think I am quite a way from them but suddenly I feel a tongue licking my arm like a strong, wet massage. Philip is laughing. 'Their tongues are much longer than you think, aren't they? And they are very curious animals, always wanting to know what is going on.' One or two are almost clambering over each other to get a view of the strangers walking in front of them. 'Not sure about their brains, though, not sure where *they* are…'

Daniel is having no trouble at all photographing them as they lunge towards his camera. They just might eat it, that's the only thing. Or plant a great wet kiss on the lens, which would be very sticky to get off.

Top: Each of the heifers has a face as individual as can be.

Above: High nutrient food pellets at feeding time.

'What breeds are these, Philip?' I ask.' You said you had Friesians onetime.'

'See the lighter black and white ones? They are Friesians. Mostly, though we have gone over to Swedish Red and Swiss Brown crosses. They tend to be a bit hardier – feet can be a problem with cattle, if they get an infection or whatever. They are also better for beef.'

The colours – black, brown, fawn, rich rust, bronze and white - are almost infinite in their subtlety and variety. Each beast also has a face as individual as a human. 'Look at this one,' says Philip, as one heifer, not very old, is trying to clamber and push her way towards us. She has the most beautiful shades of orangey-brown, and almost auburn hair on her head, which is topped with wonderful big furry ears. 'Looks more like a teddy bear.' It's true and we can't help laughing.

On the other side of us are two huge, utterly magnificent, beasts which are waiting to calf and have a large area all to themselves. They are more like small buses. 'You have to be careful,' warns Philip. 'Once they calve, they can be protective. Get too close, one flick of their neck and you're down.'

We are lucky to come at feeding time. The herd is first fed special nutrient-packed food pellets in long stone troughs; then silage made on the farm, to fill them up. Can cows overeat? 'Indeed, they can. We have to be a little careful about that,' Philip explains.

'And the calves, when they are very young, do they have extra rations?'

'Sure, they do. Come and see.'

Philip leads the way into a separate part of the shed where young calves are held. Milking has begun and two youngsters, Jake and Robert, are busy taking pails of the freshest milk possible over to them. It is difficult to place the pails in the proper slot as the animals are so keen to get on with things that they seem to want to eat the bucket.

A couple of other members of the Norton clan arrive and set to work, including David, who oversees everything here. 'Family,' says Philip. 'At times like milking, it is all hands on deck.'

Or, as he said to us before, you are born into it. It's a life.

Grateful thanks to Emily Norton who has provided us with this wonderful recipe.

BUTTERMILK PIE

This is a great recipe for Buttermilk Pie adapted from the Hairy Bikers TV show. Buttermilk is the liquid part that separates away from the solid butter when we churn our Norfolk Butter. It makes a great marinade as it is slightly acidic, but can be used in many baking dishes too. This recipe is incredibly simple and very effective, combining the great tastes of vanilla and lemon in a light custardy, swirly mix. If you are having a 'Delia cheat' moment, simply use a pre-made pastry base or you can use a crumbled biscuit base like for a cheesecake. Delicious!

Ingredients:
1 cup/250ml Nortons Dairy Buttermilk
1 teaspoon vanilla extract
1 cup caster sugar (this quantity makes it very sweet - use less if you don't have such a sweet tooth)
100gms Nortons Dairy Norfolk Butter, softened
5 eggs
2 tbsps/30gm plain flour
1 lemon - juice and rind
1 large pastry shell

Method:
Pre-heat oven to 200 degrees C. To make, simply cream the butter and sugar together, then add the eggs one at a time. Add the remaining ingredients and pour into the pastry shell. Cook for 10 minutes, then turn the oven down to 180 degrees C and cook for a further 40 minutes, or until firm. Serve with a sprig of mint and fresh whipped double cream (Nortons Dairy, of course!).

ALCHEMY AND SCIENCE – THE ART OF MAKING THE PERFECT CROISSANT

AS IT HAPPENS, I HAD just returned from Hong Kong on a well-known airline several days before meeting Grimsby. Now it is fair to say that airline food is not going to win many awards – especially not in Economy Class: in fact, if you are not good at catching as the cabin crew rush past you and virtually sling it at you, you may miss it altogether. Thus it was with my 'breakfast' a couple of hours before landing in London. I am sure I detected a faint snarl on his face as the young flight attendant chap issued the immortal word 'Enjoy!'

There is a yellow paste. Custard? For breakfast? No, surely not, for I have been to a reasonably good boarding school and know that custard does not come with green flecks in it, and also accompanied by half a withered tomato. Ah! It dawns: this must be scrambled egg, Spock, but not as we know it. I swear it gives a slight shudder. Alongside is a curious horseshoe-shaped thing that is very hard. 'Pardon' (oh why am I always so lily-livered with cabin crew?), I say, 'what is this, please?'

'That, Sir, is a croissant. It's French.'

'Really,' I reply with a pathetic smile. 'I thought it was something to keep by us to bash the windows in with should the worst come to the worst and we landed in the ocean…'

Before the day is out I am to learn the art of the croissant, courtesy of 'Grimsby' who owns and runs Pye Bakers, just off the Aylsham Road in Norwich. He is a tall, healthy looking chap with his hair swept back in a ponytail and he welcomes Daniel and I with a big smile. We had previously met him and his partner, Sally, on the first day of the Bidwell's Norfolk Food Festival in the Forum where they had a stall selling an array of their cakes, pastries and breads. It was first thing in the morning and business was so brisk that we arranged to return in a few hours when things might be a tad quieter. This was a mistake as, by the time we got back at about 2pm, they had completely sold out of their day's stock and had to

A beaming Grimsby tempts us to a basket of his 'just-baked' bread.

'It is all very tempting, but what shall I buy?' Sally and Grimsby (right) chat to customers at the annual Food Fair in Norwich.

rush the van back to the bakery for fresh supplies. 'Best come and see us in the bakery,' Grimsby had said. 'We'll have time to talk there, and I can show you how we make things.' And so here we were.

First off, the tour. Sally joins us as he takes us round. There are two units now, although he started off with just the one about three years ago. 'I was lucky as it was already a food business, so I was able to buy a lot of the equipment,' he says. In the first unit are three other guys, including Rob who has been friends with Grimsby for many years.

'Eons, actually,' says Rob with a mock grimace. 'When Grimsby decided to start his own business, my wife and I threw in our lot with him.' He is currently throwing circles of pastry about, gently but with intense concentration, no doubt for alchemic bakery reasons which escape me and Daniel, before lining cases ready for filling with goats' cheese and red onion quiches.

Santa's Elves

I wonder how many people are employed here? 'Eight full time.' And the hours of operation? 'Pretty much, 24 hours a day, five and a half days a week. There are a couple of hours when things slow down a bit. We start at 1am in the morning.' It is a lovely image – we had noticed on coming up that someone passing by would have no idea, from the outside, that anything was going on here. Yet here are dedicated experts producing the pride of Norfolk breads and pastries around the clock.

We pass into unit number two. There are ovens here that are, frankly, big. I mean, pretty massive, bigger than me and I am six foot. As wide again. There is another, not very hot but kept at the requisite temperature for allowing things to mature and rise, that is full of Italian Panettone Every twenty minutes or so in our subsequent visit, Rob or Grimsby himself will check them to see if they are 'just so', ready for their next stage. One time, Rob thinks they are perfect but Grimsby is not so sure. 'Just maybe five more minutes?' They look luscious with fruit bursting out. I, like lots of us, have bought these Panettone on my way back from Genoa airport or wherever on our Italian holiday. They were always dry, to my way of thinking, and not very nice. Can I touch one in the oven? 'No, no, please don't do that,' says our host. 'They will collapse. Later, when they have been 'cut' at the top – if you didn't do this they would explode, so we go for a sort of controlled blow-out – we can taste them. A top chef in London introduced me to the best way to eat it – with lots of Torta di dolcelatte, which is layers of mascarpone and dolcelatte cheese.'

Rob is a picture of concentration as he works on his pastry rounds.

UGLY CHOCOLATE PUDDING

Grimsby has specially created the following luscious pudding for us.

Ingredients:
150g Self-raising flour
100g castor sugar
2 tbsp good quality dark cocoa powder
125ml milk
1/2 teaspoon vanilla extract
50g melted butter
1 egg
70g dark chocolate drops or chopped bars (60-70 % cocoa solids)

For the Sauce:
150g light soft brown sugar
2 tbsp good quality dark cocoa powder
50g butter melted
375ml boiling water

Method:
Preheat oven to 175 degress C.

You will need a baking dish or roasting tray, which will hold 1.5 to 2 litres of water.

Try this out before you start to put your pudding together or you may have a bit of oven cleaning to do afterwards. If not you could always halve the recipe.

Lightly butter dish.

In a bowl sieve flour, sugar and cocoa. Add to this the chocolate drops, milk vanilla extract, egg and melted butter, and whisk all these together to make a batter.

Pour this in to buttered baking dish and give dish a light tap on the table to even out the mixture.

In another bowl sieve cocoa for sauce and mix with light brown sugar. Sprinkle this over the pudding batter in dish. Mix melted butter and boiling water together and pour all over the pudding.

Put this in to the oven of 35-40 minutes.

To test that it is cooked stick a skewer in the middle of the pudding - when drawn out there should be no sign of batter.

There will be at the bottom a rich dark chocolate sauce. Let pudding stand for 10 minutes before serving. I would serve with either crème fraiche, pouring cream or vanilla ice cream.

Grimsby hails from fine Scottish folk. He has been a chef all over, notably in London where he worked with many well-known people, including Antony Worrall Thompson. He has an infectious enthusiasm and sense of humour and, I suspect, could entertain with tales of fine food and the eating thereof until the building fell down. Sally used to run a media monitoring agency and they met up at the opening party for one of Grimsby's restaurants in London. 'At the time, I would have gone to the opening of an envelope, so it was a very run-of-the-mill evening,' she explains, laughing. She makes a very slight figure with long blond hair. I cannot help wondering what her first impression of Grimsby was?

'My first thought was that I was not interested in a fat chef.' This is, incidentally, not at all fair but Grimsby likes to share the joke.

Grimsby considers the Panettone is perfect now.

Top: Filling the award-winning mince pies.

Top centre: 'And finally' – shaking sugar on to the mince pies before baking.

Above: A Pye Bakers' mince pie in all its glory.

Left: Putting the pastry tops on the mince pies.

'There has to be room for sampling,' he said, patting the front of his blue and white striped apron. 'Then, after a few beers I was able to point out that she wouldn't want to go out with a thin one!' The evening was a success in more ways than one and the ensuing partnership of fine chef's skills and media savvy knowledge led, after a few adventures, to the setting up of 'Pye Artisan Bakers' in Norwich about three years ago.

It is a business very much on the upward spiral. To begin, Sally would need to phone round and sell. Not now as everything is produced solely to order. 'We started three years ago and, as an example, sold maybe 300 of our luxury mince pies. This Christmas, we will produce 3500.' They recently won the Eastern Daily Press Award for the best luxury mince pies.

Sally has organised coffee for our chat and tour. There is something missing. I used to be a bit shy, but age has taught me. 'Well, we couldn't possibly comment unless we *tasted* a minced pie.'

Grimsby goes to an enormous fridge – more like a small room – and, emerging, offers Daniel and me a beautiful, deep, small pie. It is about an inch thick with a teeth-defying coat of frosted sugar on top. 'You guys are shameless, aren't you?' (frankly, Yes). 'These are some I produced earlier.'

We munch. The pastry is shortcrust but sweet. 'Some manufacturers use pastry that is either soft, mushy and tasteless or hard and sour. It has to be both short and sweet,' says the chef.

Into the mince pies go oranges, lemons, sultanas, currants, brown sugar, candied peel, spices and lots of brandy and rum.

Preparing pastry cases for the quiches.

The top sugar produces an effervescence on the tongue. And the filling which is amazing and sends little bits of taste exploding all over the mouth. What's in that? 'Well, you've got oranges, lemons, sultanas, currants, brown sugar, candied peel, spices and lots of brandy and rum.'

Daniel has all this time been getting his camera ready and experimenting with various lenses. It is hot in here and he is probably selecting one with a built-in windscreen wiper as we are very keen to picture some of the wonderful, sweet-smelling aromatic focaccia bread as it cooks. We know, because Rob has just inspected some in one of the massive ovens. Wafting around us as the oven door is opened is a heavenly smell of fine roasting dough, olive oil and rosemary. But there is something on his mind.

'Grimsby – the name. Very unusual – what's that all about, then? I mentioned to my Fiancee, Ali, that we were going to see Grimsby today, and she thought Steve and I would be going to a place in Lincolnshire!'

'Don't mention it,' (so we won't, except to the esteemed readers of this book and their family and friends and their dog and…) 'but my name is really John Watt. It's just that, in London, I got the nickname 'Grimsby' as that is where I had come from. And it stuck! Now people know me as 'Grimsby' so…'

This leads me to enquire: 'Pye Bakers? Where is that from?'

'I am a bit of a food historian. In medieval times 'Pye' was the singular of 'Pies'. Norfolk was famous for supplying the King with 100 items of 'Pye' each year, each one containing a herring. It was a kind of tax. So I decided to call my new enterprise 'Pye Artisan Bakers', the 'Artisan' bit to denote that each product was lovingly made.'

Re baking bread: Grimsby is adamant that there is nothing terribly hard about it. 'We have just lost the *idea* of trying to make breads and pastries at home. I would love it if the people of Norfolk rediscovered the lost art of creative baking. If you make a mess getting down and floury, good on you. I remember when I was a kid and I got flour and things all over the kitchen floor, my Dad said "That's fine, son – after all, that's what kitchen floors are for!"'

FOCACCIA BREAD

Here is a recipe from Grimsby for fabulous focaccia bread:

Ingredients:

Dough:
750g Strong Organic Flour
20g Fine sea salt
15g Fresh Yeast
525ml Tepid Water
17g Castor Sugar
35ml Extra Virgin Olive Oil

Topping:
Fresh Rosemary
Cherry Plum Tomatoes
Extra Virgin Olive Oil
Course Crystal Sea salt

Method:
Put water and yeast together in a large bowl, then whisk in a handful or 2 of the flour to get a runny batter. Cling film the bowl and leave to prove for 1-2 hours. In this time it will raise and bubble. This is known as a sponge.

In a second bowl put the remaining flour, fine sea salt and sugar: add to this the sponge and the olive oil. Mix these together with your hand or a wooden spoon, till a wet dough is formed, do not be tempted to add more flour as the dough should be very wet. You will need to beat the dough for about 10-15 minutes till it becomes very elastic. When the dough has become elastic pour a little olive oil over the top and cover with the cling film again. Leave the dough to prove for 1 hour and rest.

The dough will double in size.

When the hour has passed punch the dough down and put into a large roasting tray which has been rubbed with olive oil. Pour a little more olive oil over the top and press out the dough to cover the bottom of the tray. The dough should be about 1 inch thick at this stage. Stab the ends of your fingers into the dough to leave lots of little dips and holes.

Now pick the leaves off the rosemary and put on the top of the dough and cut the tomatoes in half length-ways to show that they are plum tomatoes and put these on the top cut side up. Put as much or as little topping on as you feel, there is no wrong amount. Drizzle the top with yet more olive oil and sprinkle with crystal sea salt. I would not go too heavy on the salt - just a light sprinkle goes a long way. Leave this to raise for about 1 hour or till it is very well risen and has bubbles on the surface.

Bake at 185 degrees centrigrade for about 30 minutes.

The top should be a light brown and the bottom should be firm and not soft - if it is soft pop it back in the oven for 5 minutes longer.

Carefully remove from roasting tray (I slide a small wire rack under the bread and lift it out). Cool on a wire rack if you can wait that long.

Try other toppings on your Focaccia. It lends itself well to lots of flavours. Happy Baking!

There was a wonderful aroma in the bakery as the Focaccia bread with rosemary came out of the oven...

Grimsby sets to work
on the pastry.

Opposite: Rolling the
pain au chocolat.

Something else about this second unit is that it has a glass shop front on it, behind a shutter at the moment. For this is to become a café hopefully as there are lots of people working hereabouts who could do with some daily sustenance. 'It will be a *working* bakery shop, where people can see everything being made and check out the organic ingredients before they buy.'

I wonder exactly what they will offer? 'The full range that we do now. Firstly white and granary breads then, flavoured breads developed just by us. One of our current favourites is confit garlic bread: this is where we slowly cook garlic in balsamic vinegar, herbs, sugar and olive oil for five hours which takes away all bitterness – the resulting cloves, introduced into the dough, produces little gems of sweetness and flavour which explode on your tongue. And pesto bread with homemade pesto, not shop-bought paste (basil, pecorino cheese, garlic and olive oil if you want to try to make it at home). And croissants, of course.

Ah! Croissants – I am pleased we got back to them, but they have never really taken off in England, have they? I remember my airline experience.

Grimsby takes a deep breath and is about to impart the secret of a good croissant. I just wonder if he minds giving away his best secrets in our book? 'Not at all – all the best ideas are nicked anyway. Besides, if we can produce a better "baking culture", then we will all be the winners.'

'So?'

'A fine croissant depends on the pastry which must be allowed to develop in its own time. You have to let it ferment, laminate, it must be turned, cooled down, relaxed, folded with butter and proved. It takes about two days. The one you experienced mid-air was probably fully made inside two hours. You should only eat about half of a good croissant.'

'Why's that?'

He laughs out loud. 'Because the other half will be all over your front, crispy and buttery and a bit of a mess – it will fall apart! Come, let me show you - I am about to make some pain au chocolate which uses the same recipe.' We go back to the first unit where it is wonderful to see him handling the dough. 'If you look carefully, you can see all the layers.'

As he works, we talk about bread making. Is it realistic to expect folk at home to make

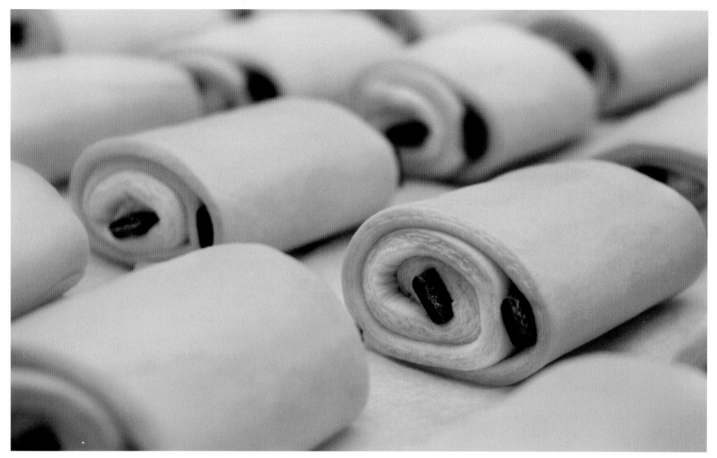

Pain au chocolate. The pastry used in the same as for croissants and takes two days to prepare – the many layers can be seen here.

bread?' Of course it is. Look, all you need for good bread is organic flour, water, yeast, salt – this inhibits the yeast – and butter, lard or olive oil. Mass-produced bread can have all sorts of other things in it like improvers, stabilizers, and bread fats, and, believe me, if you saw a lump of bread fat you would not want to eat it!'

'What is that, just coming out of the oven now?'

'That is bread made with red onion marmalade and rosemary. It is coated in sea salt. Can't let you try it, I am afraid as it is for a special order!' This turns out to be Grimsby's little joke, as he watches our crestfallen faces. Then he says: 'Like to try it?'

'OK, in the interests of book research.' We try. 'It is all right.' That is our joke, also. It is the most flavoursome, light and juicy bread on this earth. Sweet, full of flavour, and piquant all at the same time. Everyone has had rosemary and most have had sea salt, but together they blow your taste buds.

'What is your favourite bread, Grimsby?'

'Oh, all of them. Say though, I love Sourdough bread – on my day off I get up and eat toasted Sourdough bread with marmalade for breakfast. It is so simple and a real treat, and it seems to get better after a few days.'

'Do you keep bread in the fridge?' I know people have strong opinions one way or another.

'No, you don't. Fridges dry out bread. The best place for bread is in an old-fashioned breadbin. A good loaf will last several days. Then you can toast it. Wonderful!'

As we talk, there is a shift in the pace of things. Hotting up. A few new workers come in, scrub up and get down to what is obviously very hard work. Yet, for all this and the rapt concentration, there is a keen enjoyment in what is going on.

Sally has been absent, phoning for orders from the front office. She has a farmers' market to attend next day.

She comes in with a notepad. 'Please can we have carrot cake, fruit walnut cake, classic chocolate cake and, maybe some beetroot and chocolate cake? Then I need 200 mince pies for Aylsham. Then some lemon pies and Norfolk Treacle Tart – the Blumenthal recipe but heavy on the real treacle, not so much golden syrup. And, Grimsby, a customer mentioned that you talked to her about a parsnip cake. Can you do that?'

'Yes, give me an hour or so.'

The place is a'buzzin. Santa's Elves are very happy and very busy.

Daniel and I melt away. What a privilege it has been!

GOO AND GAA AND OTHER GOATS

IT IS PROBABLY TRUE TO say that fine cheeses are not products that spring immediately to mind when thinking of Norfolk Foods. Yet, here, as in other areas of eating, there has recently been much to become excited about.

Sam Steggles and his brother, Bertie, are showing us around his goat milking and cheese-making facilities in Ellingham. Daniel and I are talking to Sam whilst his 24 goats bustle, butt and occasionally jump – they are proficient jumpers, goats – around us. Most are British Saanen and white but two, of a light brown hue, are British Toggenburg. 'These two belong to my young son, William.' He says. 'They are called 'Goo' and 'Gaa', as those are the only words William knew when we introduced them to him.'

They are inquisitive and like human contact, unlike some creatures we have recently met, like Steve Childerhouse's geese who waddle, skip and flap off to the most distant place possible when a human is in view. They particularly like to munch at anything in reach. One pulls at Daniel's shirt from behind as he crouches down to get a good pic, another finds the camera bag a bit tasty and, hey-ho, there, over into the straw, goes the tripod I was careless to leave unattended. They like to be patted and stroked, and will sometimes raise their undeniably pretty faces to you to ask for more attention.

Also, they value routine. We have come at the time of the afternoon milking which is done twice a day, at about five in the morning and the same time pm. As Sam and Bertie arrive, they start to gather at the gate leading to the milking parlour – about ten yards away in this case.

Daniel asks about other animals. 'Yes, things go together. When all is done, there is a whey left which makes excellent food for pigs. We have two pigs at the present.' Sam leads him towards a separate small building alongside the goats. 'Meet my two pigs, 'Apple' and 'Sauce'.'

Sam and his brother,
Bertie, amongst their goats.

Most of the goats are
British Saanen.

Once they are back, I ask Sam 'Why goats?'

'I have always loved animals in general. When I was 12, I was given a Jersey cow for Christmas. I remember, one Christmas morning, getting down to the living room. The curtains were closed on the French Windows leading out to the garden. Mum asked me to open them and, lo!, there in the garden was a Jersey cow with a red ribbon around its neck. It was for me!'

Thereafter, there was no doubt as to his future career path. 'But goats; that came a bit later. I had been intrigued by goats and it was a fine way to start a business without massive expense as I did not have a cheque book to buy a major farm. And, there was not any other producer of goats' cheese in Norfolk that I was aware of.'

The goats are being milked by this time, each in their pen and each simultaneously munching away contentedly at their food pellets.

The brothers have just the
two pigs at the moment, but
numbers may increase.

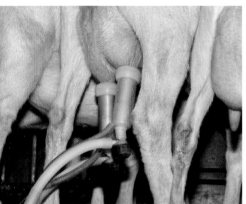

The goats are taken to the
milking parlour twice a day.

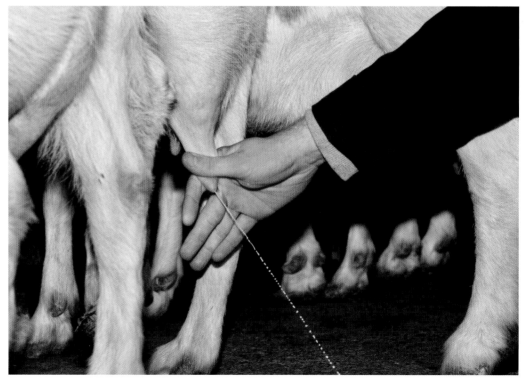

Sam takes us to the cheese-manufacturing facility. The strictest hygiene rules apply here. Wash, scrub down, put on fresh clothing, and only then take a look. Perhaps the most impressive thing about this particular cheese-making process is that the milk from the goats starts the process into cheese immediately – there is no gap in time while the milk is transported who-knows how many miles, to producers whose procedures we don't know, to shop shelves where marketing strategies are an unknown quantity. Everything is done straight away and here.

Sam takes a couple of samples out of a fridge. There is the round Ellingham Cheese and the tubular Herbie Ellingham. 'We use vegetarian rennet', he says, 'so vegetarians can eat it without any problems.'

We go back into the milking area. All is now quiet. We take a look at the goats in their indoor barn. They are settling down in clean straw, milked and very content. Their daily routine is done.

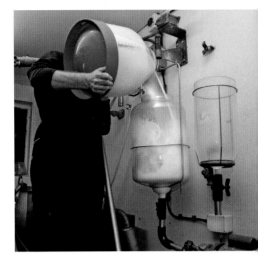

The fresh milk is filtered.

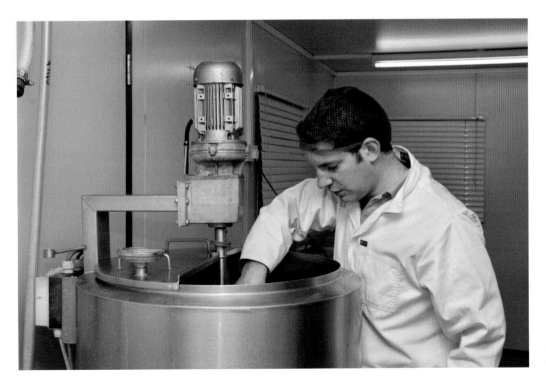

Sam in the cheese-making facility.

123

Finished cheeses

Herbie Ellingham is goats' cheese coated in herbs which provides a tasty contrast to the sweetness of grapes.

Milk and cheese produce from the goats.

'Hey, wanna come back to Fielding Cottage and try some cheese?'

In his home, Sam makes us all cups of tea. He goes to the fridge and presents a round Ellingham cheese. It is light, not at all 'goaty'. It is fresh like the morning rain when you stick out your tongue and catch a droplet. It is a bit crumbly.

Young William comes in with a handful of Christmas chocolates. He is learning to walk. 'Are you going to share them?' asks Sam. Daniel and I get one each. We put them in our pockets to have later as they don't seem to go with the cheese.

ELLINGHAM CHEESE AND MUSHROOM SNACK

Sam recommends simplicity. So take a large field mushroom, wash and grill lightly for a few minutes. Add some lemon juice. Take a round of Elliingham cheese and cut in half so you have two circular rounds of cheese. Place on top of mushroom and grill further for a few minutes. Serve with salad.

Alternatively, cut cheese into chunks and serve with salad. Yum!

Good also on pizzas in chunks and lightly grilled.

AN A-Z OF NORFOLK FOOD

A LIGHTHEARTED A-Z OF INTERESTING NORFOLK PEOPLE, FACTS, QUERIES AND STORIES ABOUT FOOD

Apples. Once the pride of our county, the apple industry has fallen from grace as species have disappeared. Happily, old varieties are making a comeback now.

Bloaters by post. Holidaymakers could once send a box of Yarmouth bloaters – salted smoked herrings – to their nearest and dearest with a 'wish-you-were-here' note, much like today you can send clotted cream from Cornwall, although I should imagine considerably less popular with the postman, and with those whose letters were transported in the same consignment.

Booze. Norfolk has always been famous for its beer. One of the most famous breweries of old was Morgans in King Street, Norwich. Tragically, the fumes were so strong that one of the Directors in Victorian times was overcome, fell into a vat, and drowned. At the other end of the scale, many impoverished folk in areas such as Coslany, made their own and sold the dubious liquid to their neighbours in an effort to make ends meet. Pubs have been having a hard time in recent years due to the smoking ban and ridiculously cheap beer available from supermarkets. Some brewers, though, buck the trend: Woodforde's, based in Woodbastwick and established in 1981, won not only the 'Best Norfolk Drink Producer' category at the 2010 Norfolk Food Festival, but also the much coveted Bidwell's Championship – ie overall top award. It has won national titles, too. Ever resourceful, the trade as a whole is bouncing back and a thriving part of the business these days is the Micro-Brewery which, although maybe selling to only one or two pubs, produces beer of a fabulous standard. The Norwich Beer Festival on October sees enthusiasts queuing around the block to gain entry to the hallowed space of St Andrews Hall to sample their latest creations: not everything put on in this medieval monastic complex is ecclesiastical in nature!

Opposite: Bloaters in a smoking oven.

Norfolk cakes – fruit tea loaf and lemon drizzle cakes.

September 2010 saw the launch also of the Norwich Wine Festival, sponsored by local businesses, to promote bars and restaurants in the region with a good wine list.

Cakes. Whilst perhaps not great bakers of bread (yet), folk are spoilt for choice when it comes to cakes. At home, the cup-cake craze of recent years has not passed the county by. It is very good for children as the basic sponge base can be quite simple to make whilst the iced top can be as imaginative as you like, often looking far too good to eat. You will see many beautiful examples on sale at farmers' markets and in farm shops, as well as more ambitious 'serious' cakes utilising local produce such as honey, apples, cherries etc. There are also a number of excellent commercial caterers who specialise in their own-recipe cakes, chocolates and sweets.

Maggie of The Redhouse Kitchen

The eyes are tempted and eating will surely follow! Some luscious cakes from Maggie of The Redhouse Kitchen.

Caleys Chocolate. Another fine Norwich firm, located once on the site of Chapelfield Shopping Centre, it survived terrible bombing in the Second World War. The firm is back now, very much on the up: as well as the chocolate, there are plans for an expanding number of cafes emanating from 'The Fine City'.

Children's events. Some events, such as the Norfolk 'highest jelly' competition each year, are pure fun and guaranteed to make the young ones think about the textures and properties of foodstuffs (although what a few add to their basic jelly mix to make it stand up does not bear thinking about!)

There is also a 'Spring Fling' in the Easter holidays at Costessey Showground where children from 4 to 14 can try their hand at making bread and sausages, watch eggs hatching and come into maybe their first close contact with birds and animals. Our own 'home-grown' chefs of the future may well become inspired here.

Colmans. Jeremiah Colman was a Victorian entrepreneur par excellence. He introduced his famous mustard in a factory down by the river in early Victorian times. He was very unusual in that he cared for the workforce in a ground-breaking way – there was an ideal village (still there) where his employees might enjoy good housing and sanitation; he appointed a medical team to care for them; and his wife, in the early days anyway, produced a nutritious lunch of stew and bread for all which cost 3d (old pennies). When he died, his funeral cortege was said to be followed by grieving crowds as large as that which attended similar evens for the great and the good in London. He is buried in Rosary Cemetery, not far from the station in Norwich.

Delia. 'Our Delia', 'The First Lady of Norwich' or possibly just 'Delia', Delia Smith is the most influential cook of modern times. Along with many others, I remember how she saved my bacon (sorry!) at Uni by teaching me that cooking is not an impossible art even for an impoverished and ham-fisted (oh dear!) student. She currently (bad to worse!) has a restaurant in Norwich Football Ground. She is a Director of the Club and has been known to stand in the middle of the pitch and demand more support from the fans when things are not going too well. 'The Canaries', as the club is known, has had many a drama over recent years and is once again on the rise. After all, you can't make an omelette without breaking eggs…

Eating well on a budget. I well remember, when I was a college teacher, that we had a catering dept that ran a very fine restaurant at lunchtimes. It was in our near neighbour county of Essex. The students were encouraged to produce food of an international standard for a moderate fee. All the local great-and-the-good came in. I was late one time, and I remember the starter offered was either garlic mushrooms or snails. 'Mushrooms are off, Sir' (they recognised me, you see, as their not-always-beloved lecturer in the very hard subject of English). 'We have French escargot, with lots of garlic. I am sure you would like that, Sir, especially cos' you always encourage us to be broad-minded.'

'Of course. Thank you, James.'

I think I was with the deputy mayor and his wife.

They got mushrooms. I didn't, and my snails had enough garlic to blow the shoes off a horse. The snails themselves were like little rubber bombs that pulverised my insides for days.

If you are out there, James, wherever you are, someday I will get you…

There are an increasing number of student-run dining rooms in our county and it is a fine way to have an excellent lunch at a much smaller cost than a meal of equivalent standard in a commercial restaurant. And, of course, it is very helpful to the students.

Farmhouse Breakfast Week. This is an event that takes place in the county in the often dark days of January when folk are encouraged to try a new type of breakfast. It is part of folklore that a good breakfast will set you up for the day: well, here, is a wonderful chance to maybe try ducks' eggs rather than chickens', or Sourdough bread as opposed to plain white (heartily recommended by Grimsby, our chef featured earlier), or maybe Liz Joint's gooseberry jam (featured in these pages, also) in place of the usual marmalade. Many restaurants will also put on special luxury breakfast packages.

Good medicine and nice smells. If you wandered the streets of Norwich a couple of hundred years ago, the stench from raw sewage chucked out of windows, to say nothing of the – by present standards – general smelliness of you fellow man, was checked by holding a cut orange to the nose. Should you be invited to attend a banquet alongside important folk – perhaps to celebrate the victory of Waterloo – it may be expected that you would wash and then cover yourself in a light coating of corn flour to which had been added a few essential oils. This absorbed the sweat and made you less obnoxious to those in the immediate vicinity.

Much of our present medicine is based on old remedies – dock leaves for an aching leg, mustard baths for headaches and colds, garlic as an antiseptic, and ginger for perking you up and banishing the blues. There is still much to the Norfolk medical folklore to be scientifically explored. In addition, new benefits for everyday foods are claimed all the time. One intriguing claim in the press recently has been for carrots: apparently even a modest extra consumption will result in your skin gaining a healthy glow, which will add to attractiveness. Well, I keep an open mind, but we have an awful lot of carrots in Norfolk and so it may be worth a go…

Harvest. There is no more beautiful sight than Norfolk at harvest time. When I was at school in Heacham, I remember the fabulous array of produce that we would bring into our local church which we kids would look at in wonder while singing 'We plough the fields and scatter the good seed on the land? And all is fed and watered by God's Almighty hand…' I didn't realize, though, that harvesting is not fixed in time but varies each year depending on the soil conditions, the weather – and we have lots of that in Norfolk – and other one-off things such as the breeding cycle of predators like rabbits (as Philip Norton makes clear in these pages). In other words it is an *art* born of long association with Norfolk's idiosyncrasies.

A classic Norfolk harvest landscape.

Corn awaits harvesting under a threatening sky.

Have a go yourself... More and more folk are growing their own food as allotments rocket in popularity, as we highlight earlier in these pages. It is also not at all difficult to make your own bread as Grimsby, our baker Food Hero, suggests.

Is? Is the Cromer Crab better than other crabs? Yes, of course it is, as Shawn tells us earlier.

Jams, juices and jellies. We would venture a guess that in Norfolk we have more small enterprises producing these than anywhere else in the land. Chilli jelly, organic apple juice, gooseberry and ginger preserve and all sorts can be obtained fresh as you like at Farmers' Markets.

Kippers. It is possible that the kipper – a split and smoked herring – was invented by accident. A fisherman by the name of John Woodger had a massive catch of herring in Yarmouth in 1850. He sold some but, not knowing what to do with the rest, he hung them in a hut, kept warm by oak chippings and sawdust, for some days. And Lo! When he returned to sort out his catch, he found he had invented something new to eat. The bloater was subsequently 'invented' – this is much the same but the complete fish is smoked and also for a shorter time.

A North Norfolk idea for cooking herring is to cut off the head, split open, and simmer for about seven/eight minutes: add lemon juice and butter (parsley butter is even better).

Opposite: The rain clouds gather but the ground is still dusty-dry – the corn must be harvested quickly.

Kippers sliced and gutted, ready to be smoked.

Alternatively, wipe with goose fat (left over in the Victorian kitchen from your goose at Christmas) and griddle or hang above the kitchen fire. As a special treat, cover with boiling beer and leave for thirty minutes: serve with egg sauce and bread.

From 1270 Great Yarmouth held a great forty-day Herring Fair, famous throughout the land. As late as 1890 Hewett's Short Blue Fleet comprised 220 smacks and fish carriers.

Lavender. Norfolk Lavender in Heacham was only founded in 1932 and now exports world-wide. Most people are aware of lavender soaps, oils, perfumes, creams and room fragrances but how many of us use it in the kitchen? It is quite strong but, used sparingly, is it fantastic. To begin, maybe dry some lavender – just hang up some fresh-cut flowers by their stalks in the kitchen – and crush the flowers into a jar of caster sugar. This can be sprinkled on ice cream, apple pie or cake. Dried lavender on its own can be stored for a year or so and can be used in all manner of savoury dishes and condiments – put some in your bread maker; mix with honey and Colman's original mustard powder for eating with beef or gammon; or experiment with other herbs – I was once in a great hurry and mistakenly made a lavender and onion stuffing rather than one with sage, and was loudly applauded around the dining table; it was only on checking afterwards that I realised what I had done (I never let on that it was a mistake, until now, of course) – and sprinkle over game or green salads.

Lavender honey is very special and sought after by aficionados, but only a small amount is produced each year and it sells out in double quick time. Sea lavender is an entirely different plant and very popular with bees and honey-makers. Regrettably, it is very hard to find now.

Mushrooms and World War Two. One of the great joys of visiting China or Taiwan is experiencing the variety of mushrooms on offer – one of the most satisfying meals I ever had was in a restaurant in the southern Taiwanese city of Kaohsiung which was famous for serving only mushrooms for every course in all their infinite flavours and textures. In Norfolk, ideal growing conditions can be found in the disused airfield buildings of the last World War. The Norfolk Flat is brilliant and maybe someday a brave entrepreneur will feel confident enough to emulate our friends in the Far East.

Norfolk Dumpling. In Victorian times, the Norfolk Dumpling got a bad reputation in some seaside resorts on the North Norfolk coast, notably Caister on Sea. Holidaymakers reported that the guest houses would provide too many at dinner time, the obvious charge

Locally grown mushrooms.

Norfolk dumplings are
fine in stews.

being that they were designed to blunt the appetite before the expensive meat course. Whatever the truth of the accusation, they are a Norfolk custom in their own right, being balls made of flour and water which are then thrown into a boiling pan for twenty minutes. They are generally eaten with gravy before a meal or with treacle afterwards. It is not considered 'proper' to use a knife and fork, but two forks only, to eat them.

Organic. Very much the current 'buzzword' in healthy food, producers such as Peter Burgess, our featured vegetable producer in Sisland, lead the way here.

Pears. We've lots to say about Norfolk apples in the chapter on 'Off to Market'. Pears, though, are also traditionally associated with the area, although a lot of trees nowadays are imports from elsewhere, like Asia. Three famous varieties which date back to the 18th and 19th centuries are the fiery-flushed, sweet and small Robin (ready for eating late summer) and grown in the county for hundreds of years; Hacon's Incomparable, medium-sized and excellent for cooking as it won't fall apart; and Blickling, which is really good for keeping and was first introduced to the world by the head gardener of the country house, Mr Allan. Learning all about the types of apples and pears at an orchard makes a great day out: The EcoTech Centre, off the A47 at Swaffham, is open 10am to 2pm and Sundays after Easter. The Norfolk Rural Life Museum boasts a complete local collection of varieties in the former workhouse site at Gressenham, just a few miles west of East Dereham on the B1146. Open most of the time, but best to give them a call first – 01362 860385. Alternatively, check them out via the website www.museums.norfolk.gov.uk

Starter idea: Robin pears, washed, served whole with Stilton cheese. Salty and sweet, crumbly and juicy, simple and rich all at the same time!

A word about Norfolk dialect: 'pear', 'pair' and 'pier' are all pronounced the same, so a visitor might look a bit confused if a Cromer resident says that 'the best place to buy a pair of pears is on the fruit stall by the pier.'

Quintessentially Norfolk food? Mustard, turkeys, chocolate, sugar, fish and chips, Samphire, organic veggies, kippers, lobsters…

Raw Food. This is a small, but increasing, movement in Norfolk, the idea being that you do not kill off essential vitamins and minerals by cooking. We have all had 'smoothies', which are fantastic, and you can make some amazing cakes. Especially good for detox, the idea is big in New Zealand. Proponents point out that, humans apart, no other species knows how to cook and they are doing just fine. But, then again, we are not prize Friesian cows (and the New Zealand cricket team has not been doing too well lately, either). Some say it can help fight disease. Fascinating stuff, but no-one would suggest that it is right for everyone and medical advice should always be sought before adopting it to a large degree.

Restaurants. 'Norfolk? Restaurants? A joke?' Not at all, although the rise of fine establishments to rival London has been so quick and impressive that many folk are taken by surprise. In Victorian times, many 'top' people fell in love with pristine communities such as Hunstanton, Cromer and Overstrand. This fell away, not helped at all by Dr Beeching, who closed many of the railways. Now we have another very welcome 'invasion' by top chefs. They may not always have known where Norfolk was to begin with – one told us that he thought Norfolk was 'somewhere on the northern outskirts of London' – but, once here, many don't want to go home. Some restaurants, such as Relish Restaurant in Newton Flotman, which won the top award in the 2010 Norfolk Food Festival for best use of regional produce, have a dedicated following. Naturally, some hark back to traditional strengths - a number of the most loved restaurants feature fish and seafood. Hence we have the Michelin-starred The Neptune in Hunstanton, Cookie's Crab Shop in Salthouse

Homegrown pears.

(going for many years, actually, but how they serve the Cromer Crab is amazing), and my personal favourite, East Runton Fish and Chip Shop. There are many more – try a stroll up St Giles Street in Norwich for more international cuisine. About ten years ago, I was in a newly established and ridiculously over-priced gastro-pub in Mayfair. On learning where I was from, our host, who ran, and still does, a very successful international media agency, said to the waiter: 'He is from Norfolk – give him a baked turnip.' Oh, revenge is sweet!

Samphire. June is the time to put on the wellies and go down to the muddy marshes of the Norfolk Coast to pick this wonderful free food. If you go to London, you'll likely get exactly the same thing with plaice or lamb but it will cost a daft amount of money as it is very trendy in Notting Hill restaurants and increasingly rare. Named after the Patron Saint of fishermen, 'Saint Pierre' because it originally grew in rocky or marshy parts of the coast, it is sometimes called 'poor man's asparagus'. It can be eaten hot with butter, cold in salads or pickled. It was also once used to make soap.

Shakespeare refers to the dangers of finding it among the rocks: 'Half-way down hangs one that gathers samphire; dreadful trade!' (Hamlet, Act IV).

Slow Food. This is an antidote to Fast Food and comes from Italy where, in the 1980s, Carlo Petrini began a war against the setting up of a fast food restaurant in Rome's historic heart. The towns taking a lead in the 'battle' are called Cittaslow towns and these include Aylsham and Diss in Norfolk. In Aylsham, it all began with a Slow Breakfast for over 100 when, in January 2005, local muesli, bread, sausages, bacon and eggs were enjoyed by all. Much to the surprise of nay-sayers, the whole thing has snowballed and there are lots of 'slow' events all year round culminating in the annual fair in October.

Smokehouses. Cley Smokehouse is one of the few remaining smokehouses in the county. Run by Glen Weston, it smokes much sought-after kippers, eels, salmon, haddock, trout, duck, bacon, prawns etc. Daniel and I were privileged to visit and watch the smoking process, which goes back several hundred years. Take herring, for example. It would come in fresh from the sea, be washed, gutted and then smoked in huge stainless steel ovens on the premises. What you got depended on the way it was treated. A bloater? Well, that is a complete fish, smoked to produce a lighter 'smoky' flavour and extremely juicy. A kipper? That is spilt, gutted and put in the smoking oven and left until it is dry but still succulent. A Red Herring? Now you are talking! This is the same fish but smoked for three weeks until it turns a distinct orangey colour. It is not for the faint-hearted, but is much beloved by local beer drinkers, amongst others, as slices go wonderfully with the local ales. In particular, as

Smoked Trout with fresh orange slices.

Top: Smoked prawns.

Above: Fine smoked salmon ready for sale.

Right: Inside the smoking oven – salmon, split kippers and red herrings can be seen here.

Kippers are hung on racks ready to be smoked.

Cley Smokehouse.

Fresh Morston mussels.

it is very smoky-strong, another pint (and another) can legitimately be requested to quench the thirst.

Bye-the-bye, this is where the term 'red herring' comes from. If you, in everyday language, speak of a 'red herring', say, in a detective story, it alludes to something introduced to throw people off the scent. This, in turn, derives from hunting. A pack of hounds, chasing the hapless fox, could be confused by a few 'red herrings' thrown on to the trail, as the scent was overwhelmingly potent. It may be an old wives tale, but convicts in Victorian times reputedly liked to throw police pursuers and their dogs off the scent in this way, though where they would have got them from is not at all clear…

There is cold smoking and hot smoking. On the whole, with the former, the food would still need to be cooked; with the latter, it could be eaten straight away.

Other foods have also been traditionally smoked – cheese, vegetables, plums and even teas.

There is still a thriving business in some countries – where the smoking is away from the main dwelling house, for smell and fire issues – in all manner of smoking appliances.

Taste Tourism. In these hard economic times, every part of the kingdom has to fight for income. In Norfolk, the finest county, we have a unique selling point in our food and food history. We have always had the best beer, chocolate, mustard, sausages, crabs, herrings, pork pies and veggies, if not always up there with the Continent in respect of our breads, pastries and wines. This latter is now being addressed in spectacular fashion. 'Taste Tourism' has become an important part of the economy.

Utterly. Can be applied to many Norfolk foods, like mustard, lobster and kippers. As in 'utterly fantastic'.

Vegetarianism. If you are creative, you can do wondrous things with the fresh, local veggies, eggs and – increasingly - cheeses. But Norfolk people don't go a bundle on processed vegetarian foods such as ham, chicken, sausages etc. There's not much of this in the shops.

Whitebait Feast. Whitebait was a great delicacy in the 19th century – there is no such fish, actually, 'whitebait' being the young and tiny sprats and herrings, which travel together in great shoals for safety. London restaurants could not get enough. Each Whit Monday until the turn of the 20th century the 'Whitebait Feast' was enjoyed all along the Norfolk Coast.

Local Victorian recipes for preparing Whitebait included pickling, smoking, boiling, frying, fermenting or eating it raw. The fishes – 'two-eyed steaks' – are extremely nutritious.

X- Factor. Well, yes, our food has that, doesn't it?

Yummy. Nuff said.

Zzz... Quite excusable after a fabulous Norfolk lunch or dinner.